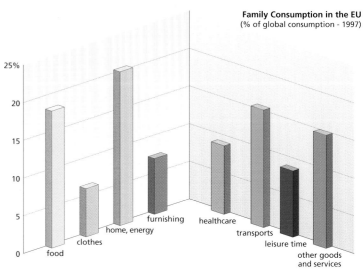

Family Consumption in the EU
(% of global consumption - 1997)

food · clothes · home, energy · furnishing · healthcare · transports · leisure time · other goods and services

Nations and Territories

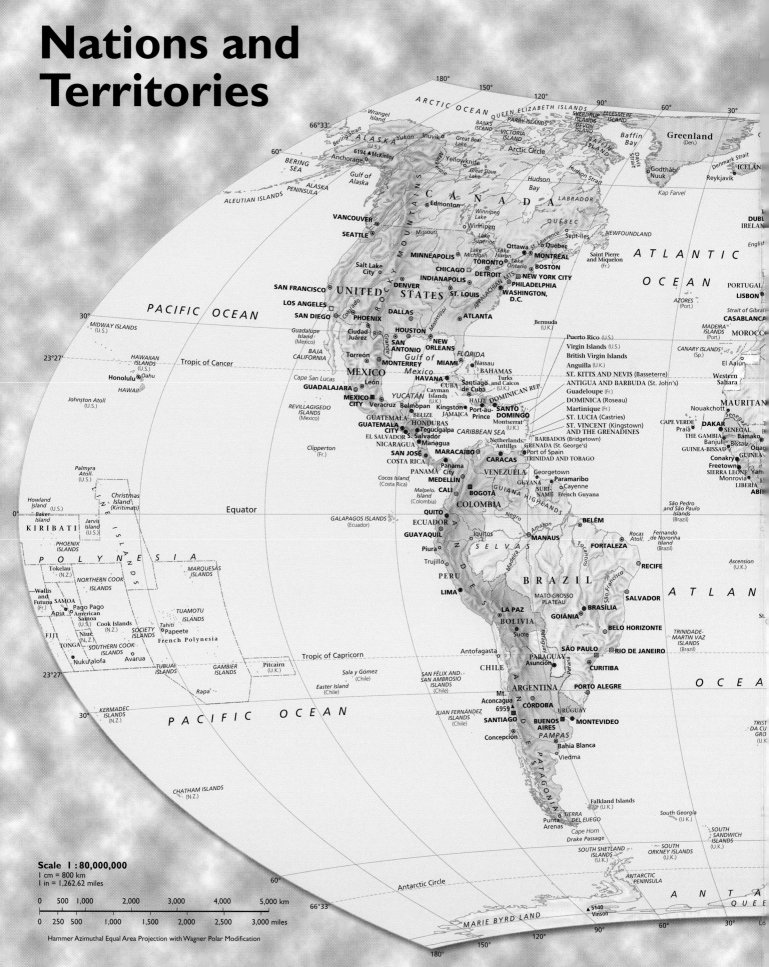

Population, Urbanism

Europe

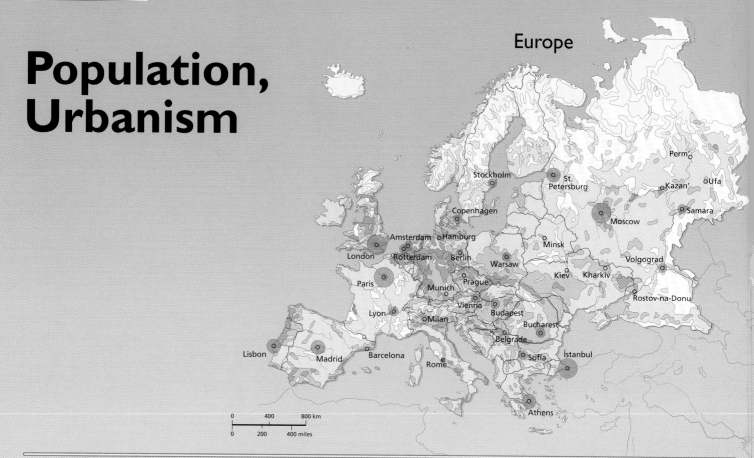

Perm'
Stockholm
St. Petersburg
Kazan'
Ufa
Copenhagen
Samara
Moscow
Amsterdam
Hamburg
Minsk
London
Rotterdam
Berlin
Warsaw
Volgograd
Paris
Munich
Prague
Kiev
Kharkiv
Vienna
Budapest
Lyon
Milan
Rostov-na-Donu
Bucharest
Belgrade
Lisbon
Madrid
Barcelona
Sofia
İstanbul
Rome
Athens

0   400   800 km
0   200   400 miles

Population density
(number of people per km²)

Europe
- [ ] 0 - 1
- [ ] 1 - 10
- [ ] 10 - 50
- [ ] 50 - 100
- [ ] 100 - 200
- [ ] more than 200

Asia, Africa and Americas
- [ ] uninhabited areas
- [ ] 0 - 1
- [ ] 1 - 10
- [ ] 10 - 50
- [ ] 50 - 100
- [ ] 100 - 200
- [ ] more than 200

Oceania
- [ ] uninhabited areas
- [ ] 0 - 2
- [ ] 2 - 10
- [ ] 10 - 40
- [ ] more than 40

People living in metropolitan areas
- 1,000,000 - 2,500,000
- 2,500,000 - 5,000,000
- 5,000,000 - 10,000,000
- more than 10,000,000

Asia

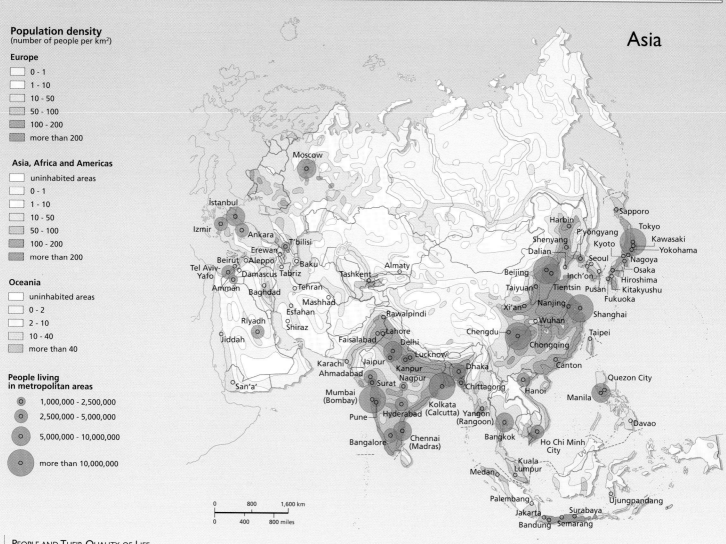

Moscow
İstanbul
Izmir
Ankara
T'bilisi
Erewan
Beirut
Aleppo
Baku
Almaty
Tashkent
Harbin
Sapporo
Tokyo
P'yongyang
Kawasaki
Tel Aviv-Yafo
Damascus
Tabriz
Shenyang
Kyoto
Yokohama
Amman
Baghdad
Tehran
Dalian
Seoul
Nagoya
Mashhad
Beijing
Inch'on
Osaka
Esfahan
Taiyuan
Tientsin
Pusan
Hiroshima
Kitakyushu
Rīyadh
Shiraz
Xi'an
Nanjing
Fukuoka
Jiddah
Rawalpindi
Chengdu
Wuhan
Shanghai
Lahore
Faisalabad
Delhi
Lucknow
Chongqing
Taipei
Karachi
Jaipur
Kanpur
Canton
Ahmadabad
Nagpur
Dhaka
Quezon City
Surat
Chittagong
Hanoi
Manila
Mumbai (Bombay)
Hyderabad
Kolkata (Calcutta)
Pune
Bangalore
Chennai (Madras)
Yangon (Rangoon)
Bangkok
Davao
Ho Chi Minh City
San'a'
Kuala Lumpur
Medan
Palembang
Ujungpandang
Jakarta
Surabaya
Bandung
Semarang

0   800   1,600 km
0   400   800 miles

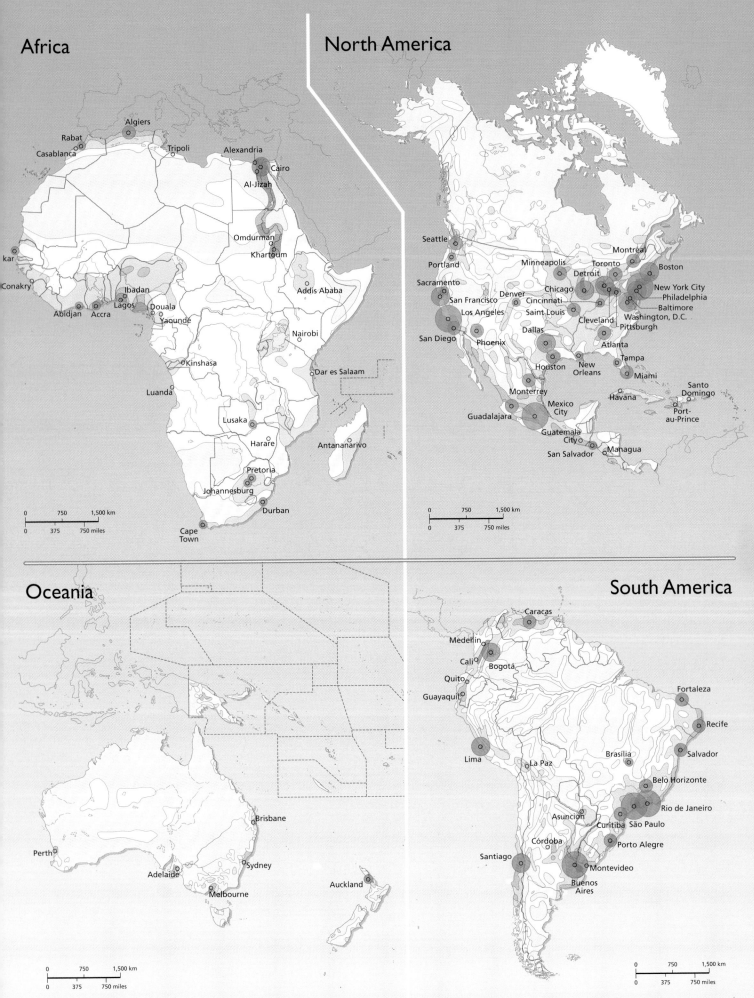

Africa

Algiers
Rabat
Casablanca
Tripoli
Alexandria
Cairo
Al-Jizah
...kar
Conakry
Omdurman
Khartoum
Ibadan
Addis Ababa
Lagos
Abidjan Accra Douala
Yaoundé
Nairobi
Kinshasa
Dar es Salaam
Luanda
Lusaka
Harare
Antananarivo
Pretoria
Johannesburg
Durban
Cape Town

0	750	1,500 km
0	375	750 miles

North America

Seattle
Portland
Minneapolis
Montréal
Toronto
Detroit
Boston
Sacramento
Chicago
New York City
San Francisco
Denver
Cincinnati
Philadelphia
Los Angeles
Saint Louis
Baltimore
Cleveland
Washington, D.C.
San Diego
Dallas
Pittsburgh
Phoenix
Atlanta
Houston
Tampa
New
Orleans
Miami
Monterrey
Santo
Domingo
Havana
Guadalajara
Mexico
City
Port-
au-Prince
Guatemala
City
Managua
San Salvador

0	750	1,500 km
0	375	750 miles

Oceania

Brisbane
Perth
Sydney
Adelaide
Auckland
Melbourne

0	750	1,500 km
0	375	750 miles

South America

Caracas
Medellín
Cali
Bogotá
Quito
Guayaquil
Fortaleza
Recife
Lima
Salvador
Brasília
La Paz
Belo Horizonte
Rio de Janeiro
Asunción
Curitiba
São Paulo
Córdoba
Porto Alegre
Santiago
Montevideo
Buenos
Aires

0	750	1,500 km
0	375	750 miles

Wealth and Poverty

Europe

Asia

Wealth distribution
GNP per inhabitant in SPP
(Standard Purchasing Power-
international dollars)

Europe
- less than 3,000
- 3,000 - 5,000
- 5,000 - 10,000
- 10,000 - 20,000
- more than 20,000

Asia
- less than 1,000
- 1,000 - 3,000
- 3,000 - 5,000
- 5,000 - 10,000
- more than 10,000

Africa
- less than 500
- 500 - 750
- 750 - 1,000
- 1,000 - 2,000
- 2,000 - 5,000
- 5,000 - 10,000

North America
- less than 3,000
- 3,000 - 5,000
- 5,000 - 10,000
- 10,000 - 30,000
- more than 30,000

South America
- less than 3,000
- 3,000 - 4,000
- 4,000 - 5,000
- 5,000 - 10,000
- more than 10,000

Oceania
- less than 2,000
- 2,000 - 5,000
- 5,000 - 10,000
- 10,000 - 20,000
- more than 20,000

- data not available
- ✳ in US dollars

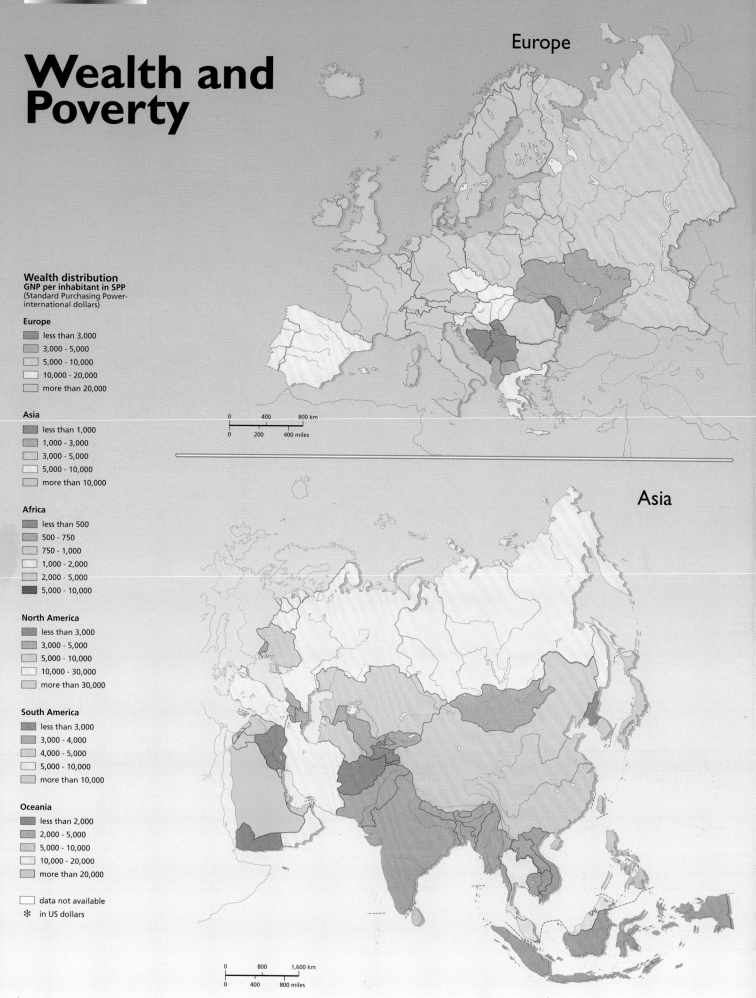

| 0 | 400 | 800 km |
| 0 | 200 | 400 miles |

| 0 | 800 | 1,600 km |
| 0 | 400 | 800 miles |

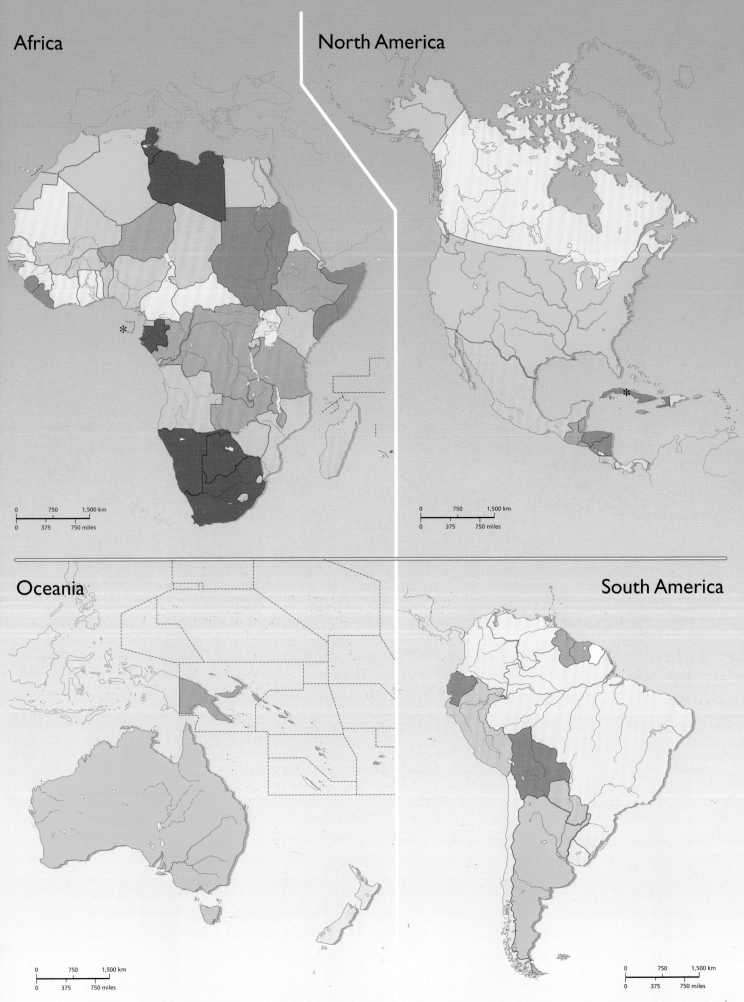

Africa

North America

Oceania

South America

School Enrollment Rates

Europe

School Enrollment Rate
Enrollments in primary and secondary schools
(% of the total number of students belonging to
the related age bracket, total percentages may
exceed 100 because of such variables as early
enrollment and repetition of grade)

Europe
- less than 80
- 80 - 90
- 90 - 100
- 100 - 110
- more than 110

Asia
- less than 60
- 60 - 70
- 70 - 80
- 80 - 90
- 90 - 100
- more than 100

Africa
- less than 40
- 40 - 60
- 60 - 80
- 80 - 100
- more than 100

North America
- less than 50
- 50 - 70
- 70 - 80
- 80 - 90
- 90 - 100
- more than 100

South America
- less than 80
- 80 - 90
- 90 - 100
- more than 100

Oceania
- less than 60
- 60 - 80
- 80 - 100
- more than 100

- data not available

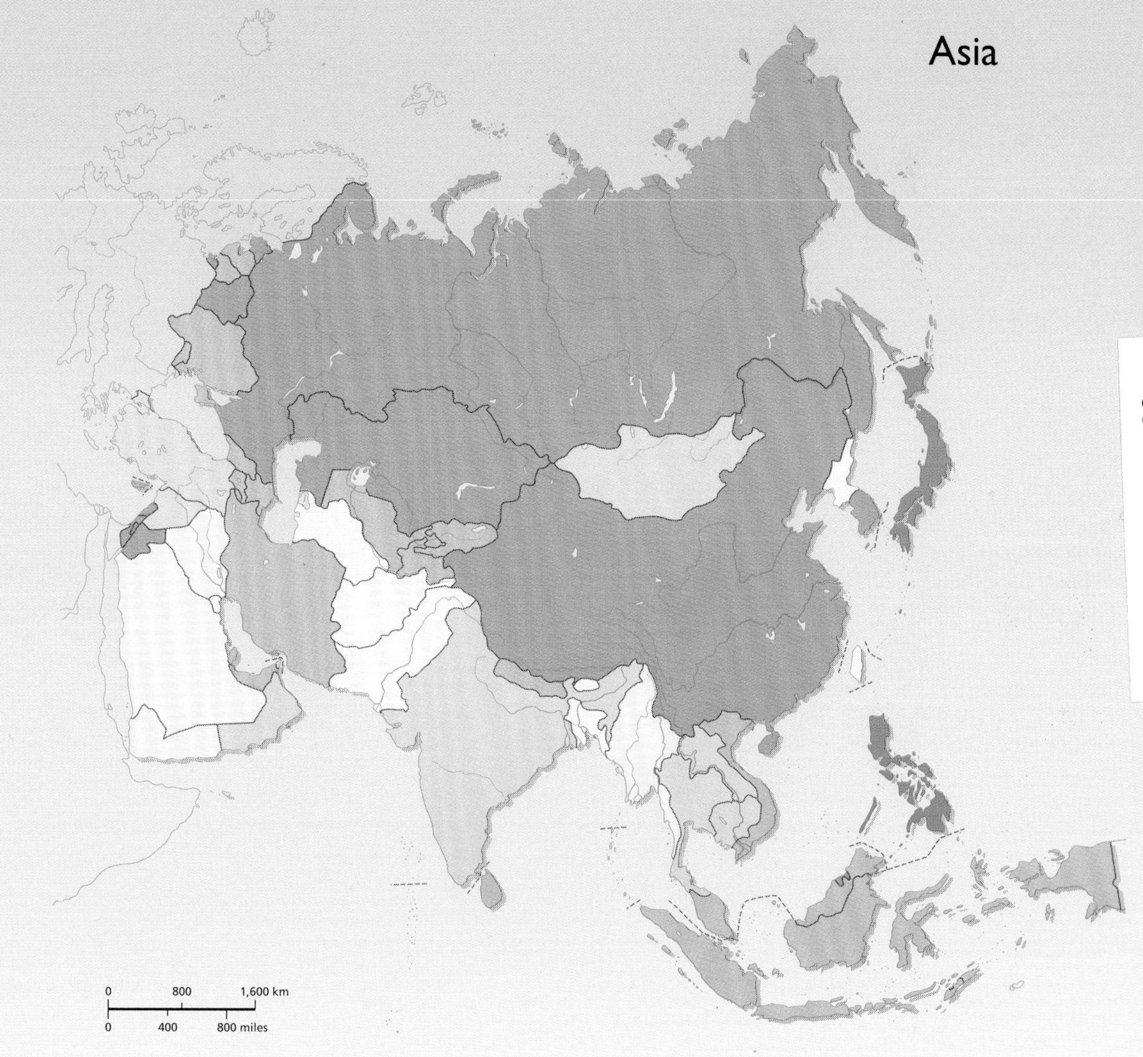

0   400   800 km
0   200   400 miles

Asia

0   800   1,600 km
0   400   800 miles

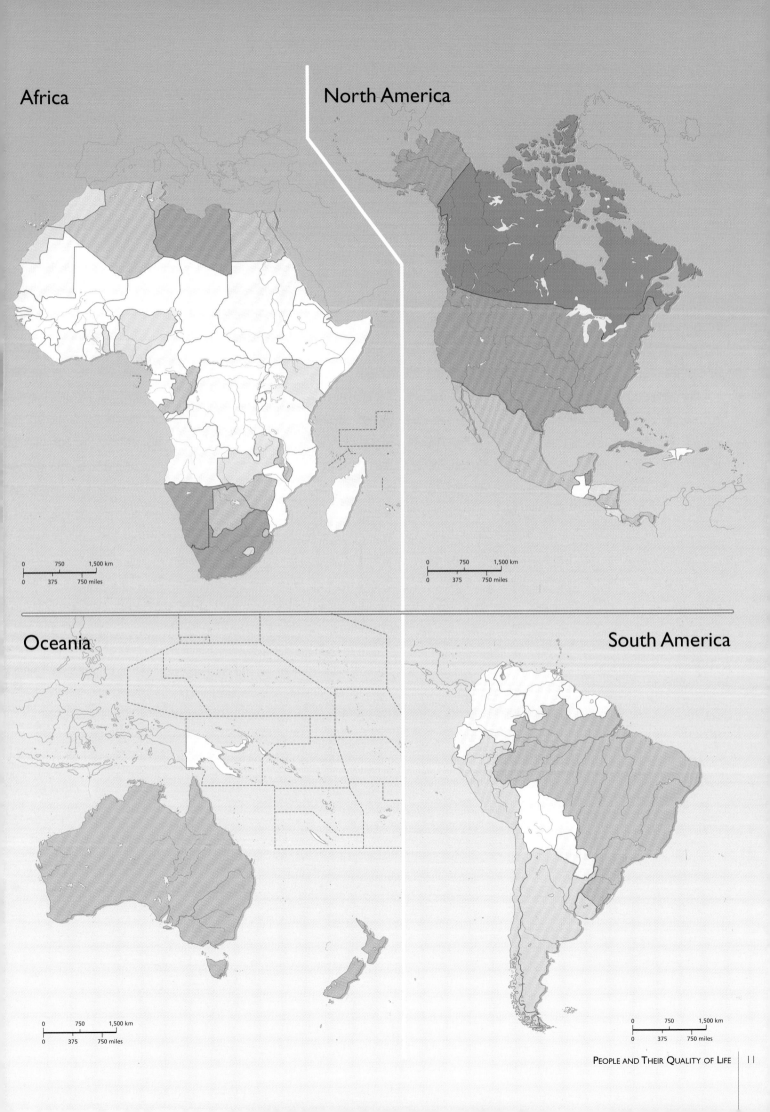

Africa

North America

Oceania

South America

0 750 1,500 km
0 375 750 miles

0 750 1,500 km
0 375 750 miles

0 750 1,500 km
0 375 750 miles

0 750 1,500 km
0 375 750 miles

Employment

Europe

Asia

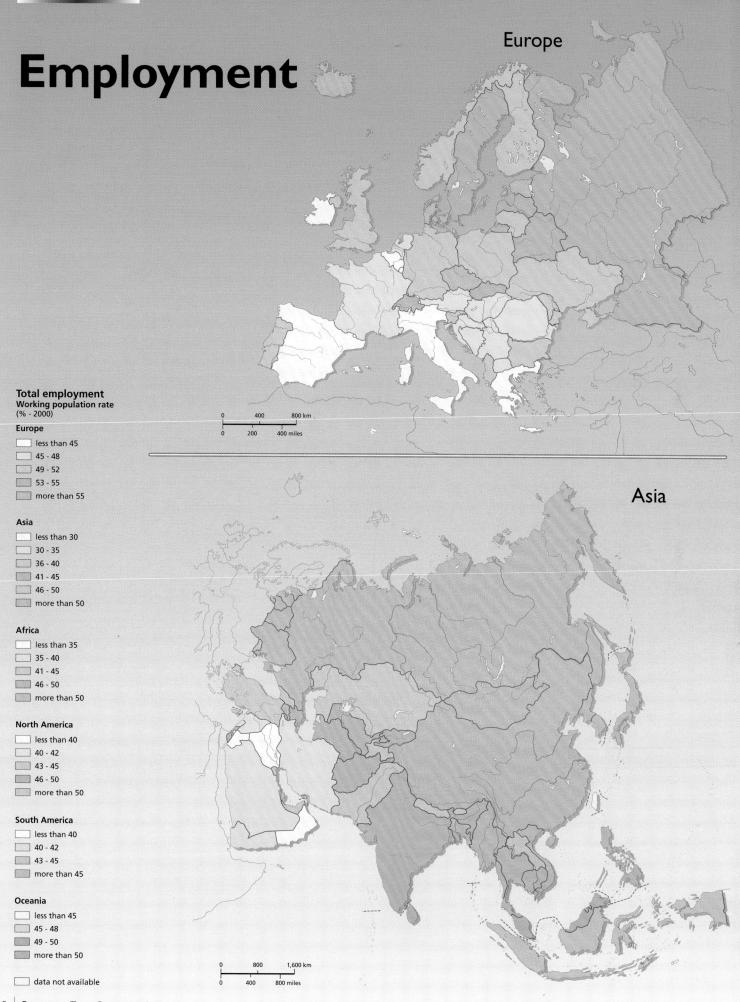

Total employment
Working population rate
(% - 2000)

Europe
- less than 45
- 45 - 48
- 49 - 52
- 53 - 55
- more than 55

Asia
- less than 30
- 30 - 35
- 36 - 40
- 41 - 45
- 46 - 50
- more than 50

Africa
- less than 35
- 35 - 40
- 41 - 45
- 46 - 50
- more than 50

North America
- less than 40
- 40 - 42
- 43 - 45
- 46 - 50
- more than 50

South America
- less than 40
- 40 - 42
- 43 - 45
- more than 45

Oceania
- less than 45
- 45 - 48
- 49 - 50
- more than 50

- data not available

| 0 | 400 | 800 km |
| 0 | 200 | 400 miles |

| 0 | 800 | 1,600 km |
| 0 | 400 | 800 miles |

Contents

People and Their Quality of Life

Please visit our web site at: www.worldalmanaclibrary.com
For a free color catalog describing World Almanac® Library's list of high-quality books and multimedia programs, call 1-800-848-2928 (USA) or 1-800-387-3178 (Canada). World Almanac® Library's fax: (414) 332-3567.

Library of Congress Cataloging-in-Publication Data available upon request from publisher. Fax (414) 336-0157 for the attention of the Publishing Records Department.

ISBN 0-8368-5618-X

This North American edition first published in 2004 by
World Almanac® Library
330 West Olive Street, Suite 100
Milwaukee, WI 53212 USA

This U.S. edition copyright © 2004 by World Almanac® Library.
Original title: *Uomo—la qualità della vita.* Italian Edition:
© GEOnext—ISTITUTO GEOGRAFICO DE AGOSTINI S.p.A., Novara, 2002
Developed by the editorial and cartographic staffs of
GEOnext - Istituto Geografico De Agostini S.p.A. - Novara

Translation by: N.C.M Servizi srl
World Almanac® Library editor: Gini Holland
World Almanac® Library cover design: Scott M. Krall

Printed in EU

1 2 3 4 5 6 7 8 9 08 07 06 05 04

Maps of Our World

People and Their Quality of Life

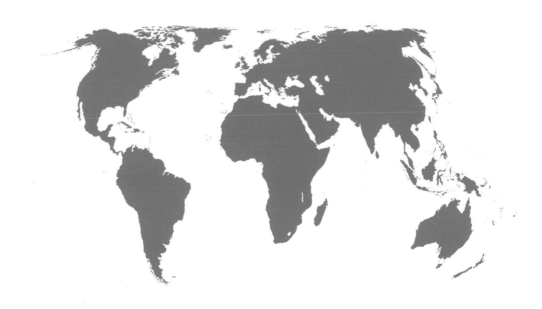

WORLD ALMANAC® LIBRARY

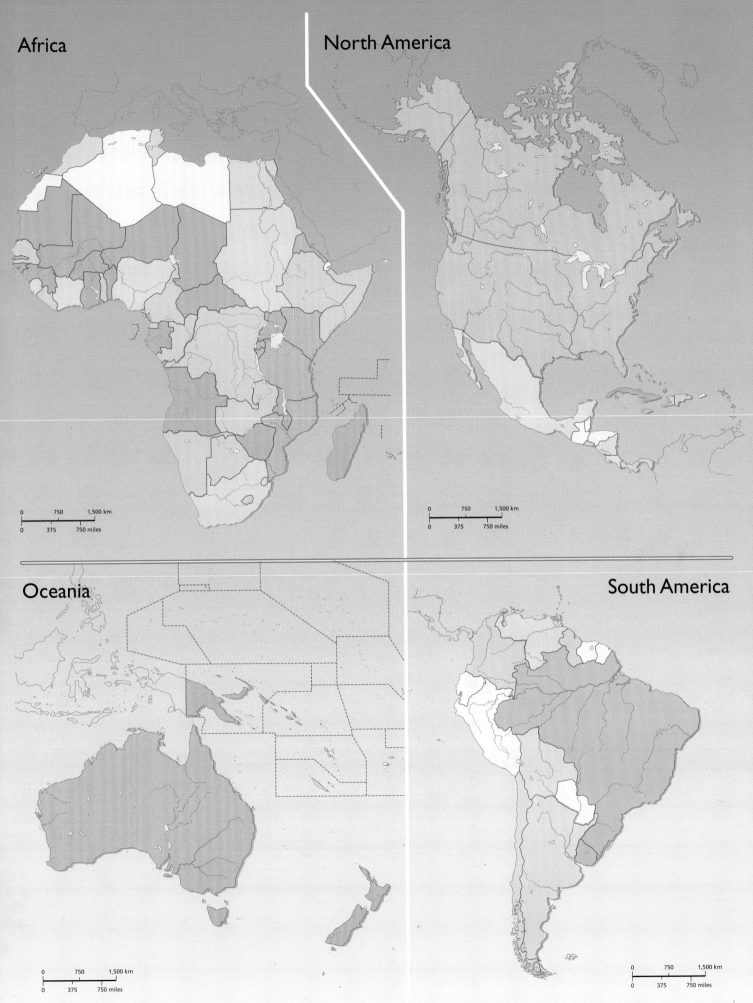

Africa

North America

Oceania

South America

0 750 1,500 km
0 375 750 miles

0 750 1,500 km
0 375 750 miles

0 750 1,500 km
0 375 750 miles

0 750 1,500 km
0 375 750 miles

Assistance and Social Welfare

Europe

Asia

Social Security
National expenditure for all kinds
of social assistance
(% of overall Government expenditure - 1994)

Europe
- 5 - 10
- 10 - 20
- 20 - 30
- 30 - 40
- 40 - 50
- more than 50

Asia and Oceania
- less than 1
- 1 - 5
- 5 - 10
- 10 - 20
- 20 - 30
- more than 30

Africa
- less than 1
- 1 - 5
- 5 - 10
- 10 - 15

North America
- 1 - 5
- 5 - 10
- 10 - 20
- 20 - 30
- more than 30

South America
- less than 1
- 1 - 5
- 5 - 10
- 10 - 20
- 20 - 50
- more than 50

- data not available

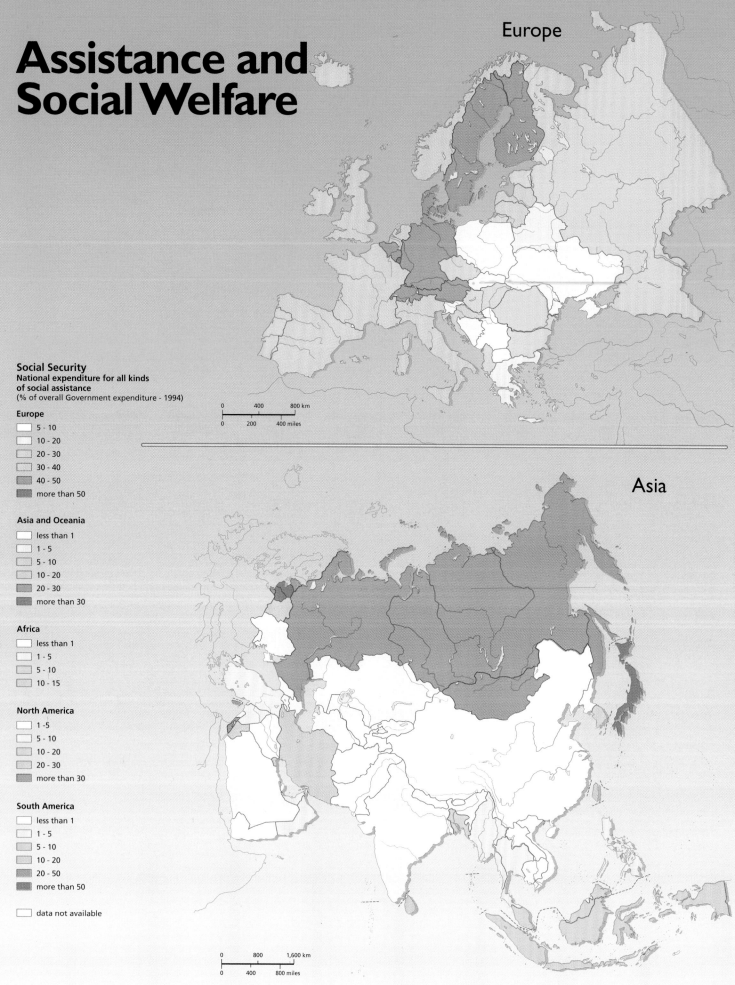

0   400   800 km
0   200   400 miles

0   800   1,600 km
0   400   800 miles

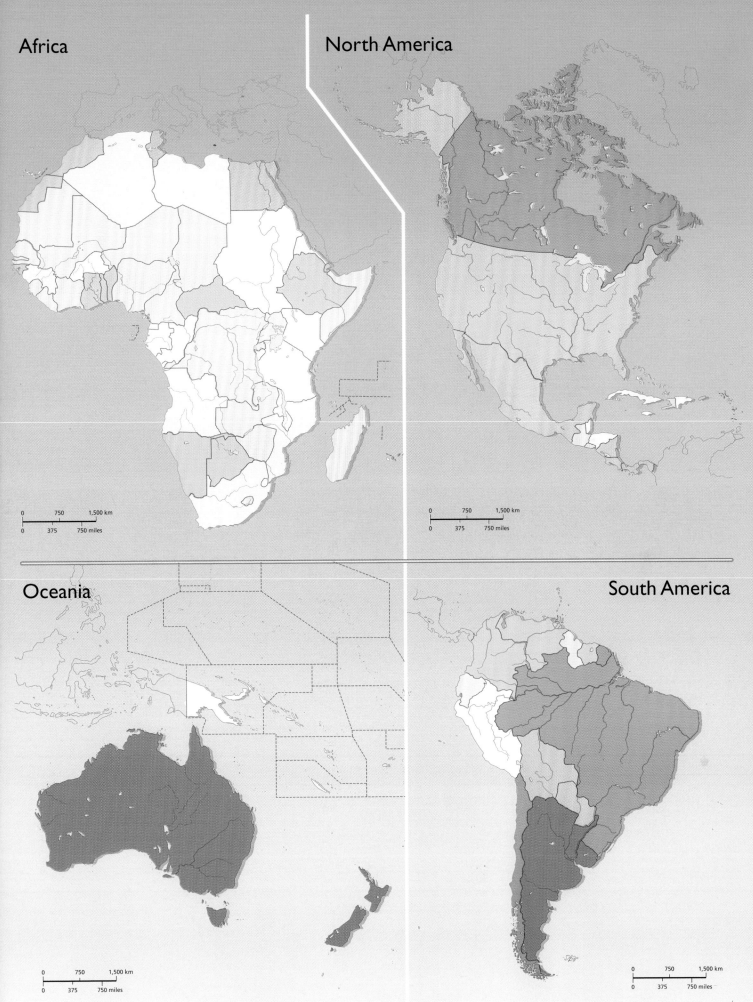

Africa

North America

Oceania

South America

| 0 | 750 | 1,500 km |

| 0 | 375 | 750 miles |

The Quality of Life
A Modern Concept

For many years, "quality of life" was defined only by economic health. In the mid-1960s, however, it became apparent that economic growth was often accompanied by social unrest and environmental problems in the industrialized countries and by serious imbalances between rich and poor countries. Quality of life, therefore, expanded to mean the well-being of a society from all viewpoints: health, housing, law and order, education, scientific progress, leisure time, guarantee of political freedom, self-respect, human rights, and, particularly in the last few years, environmental health.

Obviously, "better quality of life" has very different meanings in different countries. People living in a poor or developing country may simply wish to have enough food and healthcare, defeat illiteracy, and live longer lives. In rich societies, where primary needs are largely

met, the quality of life may be measured in relation to the possession of goods that are not vitally necessary, such as household appliances and entertainment equipment, or even a second car and home. It may also be measured in terms of available social services, quality of infrastructure, health care, political freedoms, and environmental health.

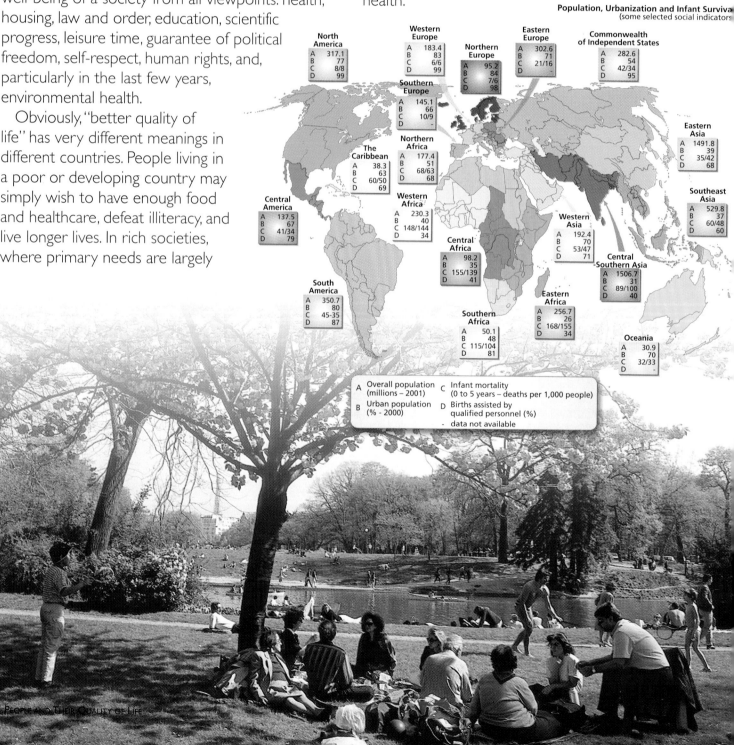

Population, Urbanization and Infant Survival
(some selected social indicators)

North America
A 317.1
B 77
C 8/8
D 99

Western Europe
A 183.4
B 83
C 6/6
D 99

Northern Europe
A 95.2
B 84
C 7/6
D 98

Eastern Europe
A 302.6
B 71
C 21/16
D

Commonwealth of Independent States
A 282.6
B 54
C 42/34
D 95

Southern Europe
A 145.1
B 66
C 10/9
D -

Eastern Asia
A 1491.8
B 39
C 35/42
D 68

The Caribbean
A 38.3
B 63
C 60/50
D 69

Northern Africa
A 177.4
B 51
C 68/63
D 68

Southeast Asia
A 529.8
B 37
C 60/48
D 60

Central America
A 137.5
B 67
C 41/34
D 79

Western Africa
A 230.3
B 40
C 148/144
D 34

Western Asia
A 192.4
B 70
C 53/47
D 71

Central Africa
A 98.2
B 35
C 155/139
D 41

Central-Southern Asia
A 1506.7
B 31
C 89/100
D 40

South America
A 350.7
B 80
C 45-35
D 87

Southern Africa
A 50.1
B 48
C 115/104
D 81

Eastern Africa
A 256.7
B 26
C 168/155
D 34

Oceania
A 30.9
B 70
C 32/33
D

A Overall population (millions – 2001)
B Urban population (% - 2000)
C Infant mortality (0 to 5 years – deaths per 1,000 people)
D Births assisted by qualified personnel (%)
- data not available

A World of Contrasts

Economic welfare and, particularly, the level of well-being of the population, divides the world into large, contrasting areas. On one side, there are developed countries, generally in the Northern Hemisphere, which record a high standard of living. These countries are highly industrialized. Agriculture is automated, services and communication networks are highly developed, there is a high level of urbanization, and the population, in general, enjoys a good income.

At the other end of the spectrum are the less-developed countries. These poorer nations are often in the Southern Hemisphere, burdened with debts, where the main problem is feeding the population. Industry is almost non-existent, agriculture is often backward, health care services are inadequate, illiteracy is widespread, the population continues to grow in spite of high mortality rates, and there is a very low standard of living.

Finally, there are developing countries. Some of them have important raw materials (like oil, copper, chromium, as well as livestock or corn), but their economies are weak. This is often because they depend on one single product. Most of their population is poor, with a very small number of rich people.

In large cities, residential areas are often next to run-down areas, where the poorest people live in inadequate housing. The poor suffer from bad hygienic conditions, lack of water, environmental pollution, and social tension, among other things.

Supermarkets and malls have become symbols of the large-scale supply of food and consumer goods in rich countries. In poorer countries, conversely, the population—mainly rural—continues to suffer serious social and economic hardships. Their living conditions often fall far below the poverty threshold, so that their main issue becomes how to get the food they need to survive .

Human Development Index
The HDI and Its Indicators

In 1990, the United Nations Development Program (UNDP) introduced a new concept and a new method to assess a country's growth, taking into consideration not only the population's income, but also its general well-being. This new measure, called the Human Development Index (HDI), focuses on three aspects of a person's main aspirations: a long, healthy life (life expectancy), acquiring knowledge (educational level), and access to economic resources (per capita income based on Gross Domestic Product, or GDP). Three groups of countries are thus identified: those with a high and medium-high human development, recording an index over or equal to 0.700; those with a medium human development, whose index ranges between 0.500 and 0.699; and the countries with a low or very low human development, recording an index below 0.499.

In most of the 162 countries considered in the Human Development Report, which the UNDP publishes every year, the HDI showed an upward trend over the last 25 years. Some countries such as Egypt, Indonesia, the Korean Republic, and Portugal recorded significant growth, while in 20 countries in Africa, Eastern Europe, and in the former Soviet Union, the index declined.

LONGEVITY AND HEALTH
↓
Life Expectancy at Birth

The possibility of living a long life is called life expectancy, which is the average number of years that a person may be expected to live. Life expectancy is one key indicator of the quality of life in a given country because it reflects the probability of good health, good nutrition, and adequate health care services.

↓
Life Expectancy Index

EDUCATION AND ACCESS TO KNOWLEDGE
↓
General school enrollment rate and literacy among adults

The level of education combines two different indicators: the adult literacy rate (the percentage of people over the age of fifteen who can read and write) and the school enrollment rate (the percentage of people enrolled in school by age group). These two indicators are combined by assigning 2/3 of the weight to the adult literacy rate, and 1/3 of the weight to school enrollments.

↓
Education Level Index

DECENT STANDARD OF LIVING
↓
Available wealth = Gross Domestic Product per person

Wealth is measured through the real per capita GDP (Gross Domestic Product), expressed in "international dollars", i.e. in Purchasing Power Parity. This latter indicator has been the most debated one at an international level, and the one which has been most significantly modified, since economic growth had been previously considered as the only development measure.

↓
GDP Index

Comparison between wealth and the Human Development Index (HDI)
(in some countries)

40 — 30 — 20 — 10 — 5 — 0

GNP/pers.
(thousands of international dollars PPP = Purchasing Power Parity – 1999)

USA, Norway, Germany, United Arab Emirates, Spain, Oman, Czech Republic, Saudi Arabia, Slovakia, South Africa, Costa Rica, Botswana, Lithuania, China, Egypt, Angola

0.2 — 0.4 — 0.5 — 0.6 — 0.7 — 0.8 — 0.9 — 1

Human Developmpent Index - HDI
(1999)

HDI =

Average value of all indexes

Life Expectancy Index

Education Level Index

GDP Index

The HDI formula is important because it extends the concept of development beyond monetary values to include health, education, and quality of life. Incomes and wealth are undoubtedly significant aspects of people's lives, but they are not the only measures.

Based on the combination of the three HDI parameters, the most developed European, Asian, and North American countries all rank at the top of the list, while African countries are at the bottom.

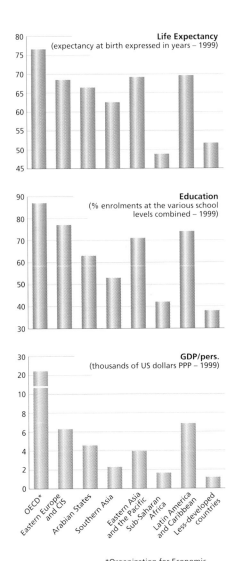

Life Expectancy
(expectancy at birth expressed in years – 1999)

Education
(% enrolments at the various school levels combined – 1999)

GDP/pers.
(thousands of US dollars PPP – 1999)

OECD*
Eastern Europe and CIS
Arabian States
Southern Asia
Eastern Asia and the Pacific
Sub-Saharan Africa
Latin America and Caribbean
Less-developed countries

*Organization for Economic Cooperation and Development

Human Development Index – HDI

Very low human development: less than 0.400
Low human development: 0.400-0.499
Medium human development: 0.500-0.699
Medium-high human development: 0.700-0.899
High human development: more than 0.900
Countries whose HDI has not been calculated

Growing Population
Where Needs Are More Pressing

The last century's considerable growth in world population was not evenly spread all over the planet. Increased population occurred mainly in large urban areas and in countries with backward economies, where resources are still scarce. In Europe, the population boom that took place between the late 18th and the mid-19th centuries had placed existing resources (agricultural produce and the first industrial profits) under such a strain that between 1850 and 1940 over 40 million Europeans had to move overseas.

Today, in many African, Asian, and Latin American countries, the sheer drop in mortality—primarily the result of considerable progress in health care—still goes hand in hand with extremely high fertility and birth rates. In these countries, population growth is not accompanied by adequate economic development. Rather, minimal economic progress is often undone by rocketing population growth. In other regions, such as the African Sahel, the very small population still exceeds the region's available resources. In both cases, the only solution for many lies in moving to richer countries.

There are also great differences in the population make up, in terms of age groups, between rich countries and developing countries. In rich countries, life expectancy has increased because of great progress in medicine, the improvement of living conditions, better education, increased use of contraceptives, and changes in social policies. At the same time, births in these countries have decreased and the majority of the population consists of adult or elderly people, supplemented by large communities of immigrants. In the developing countries, conversely, one third of the population is less than fifteen years old, while the percentage of elderly people is very low.

San Francisco-Oakland
Los Angeles-Long Beach-San Diego 14,200,000
Detroit Toronto
Montréal
Chicago Boston-Salem
New York City
New Jersey-Long Island 17,600,000
Washington, D.C.
Dallas
Houston
Philadelphia
Mexico City 19,000,000
Caracas
Bogotá
Lima
Santiago
Be Horiz
R Ja
São P 19,00
Buenos A 13,900,000

Population distribution and density
(people/km²)

- less than 1
- 1-10
- 10-25
- 25-50
- 50-100
- 100-200
- more than 200

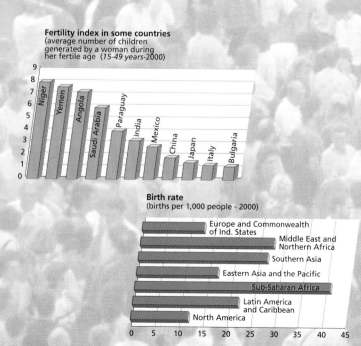

Fertility index in some countries
(average number of children generated by a woman during her fertile age (15-49 years-2000)

Niger, Yemen, Angola, Saudi Arabia, Paraguay, India, Mexico, China, Japan, Italy, Bulgaria

Birth rate
(births per 1,000 people - 2000)

Europe and Commonwealth of Ind. States
Middle East and Northern Africa
Southern Asia
Eastern Asia and the Pacific
Sub-Saharan Africa
Latin America and Caribbean
North America

0 5 10 15 20 25 30 35 40 45

The population does not grow evenly all over the world. There are countries (mainly European ones like Germany, France, and Italy) troubled by very low birth and fertility rates, which are working out economic and social incentives to encourage families to have more children. Other countries pursue birth control policies in order to be able to feed all their inhabitants and foster economic growth.

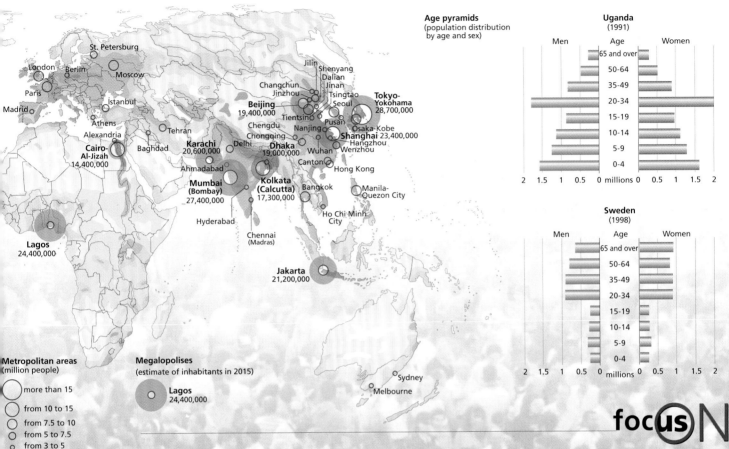

Age pyramids
(population distribution by age and sex)

St. Petersburg
London
Berlin
Moscow
Paris
İstanbul
Madrid
Athens
Alexandria
Tehran
Cairo-Al-Jizah
14,400,000
Baghdad
Jilin
Shenyang
Dalian
Jinan
Changchun
Jinzhou
Tsingtao
Beijing
19,400,000
Tientsin
Seoul
Pusan
Tokyo-Yokohama
28,700,000
Chengdu
Nanjing
Osaka-Kobe
23,400,000
Chongqing
Shanghai
Hangzhou
Wenzhou
Karachi
20,600,000
Delhi
Dhaka
19,000,000
Wuhan
Ahmadabad
Canton
Hong Kong
Mumbai
(Bombay)
27,400,000
Kolkata
(Calcutta)
17,300,000
Bangkok
Manila-Quezon City
Hyderabad
Ho Chi Minh City
Chennai
(Madras)
Lagos
24,400,000
Jakarta
21,200,000
Sydney
Melbourne

Metropolitan areas
(million people)
- more than 15
- from 10 to 15
- from 7.5 to 10
- from 5 to 7.5
- from 3 to 5

Megalopolises
(estimate of inhabitants in 2015)
Lagos
24,400,000

Uganda
(1991)

Men | Age | Women
65 and over
50-64
35-49
20-34
15-19
10-14
5-9
0-4

2 1.5 1 0.5 0 millions 0 0.5 1 1.5 2

Sweden
(1998)

Men | Age | Women
65 and over
50-64
35-49
20-34
15-19
10-14
5-9
0-4

2 1.5 1 0.5 0 millions 0 0.5 1 1.5 2

foc**us**N

Birth Control in China

China is the most heavily populated country in the world, with over 1.3 billion people. However, it is also the country that has achieved the best results in family planning. Starting in 1979, the Chinese government introduced incentives for couples having only one child, and imposed heavy fines for large families. The birthrate is now around 15.4% and the fertility rate is an average of 1.8 children per woman. In spite of this success, Amnesty International has denounced family planning in China, pointing out that it has often forced people to have abortions, sterilizations, and even (perhaps indirectly) encouraged the killing of newborns who "exceeded quotas," especially when these were girls. The country is thus facing the problem of an excessive number of males compared to females. According to UNICEF, China "lacks" 29 million girls.

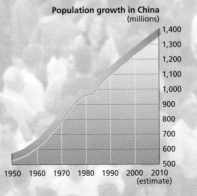

Population growth in China
(millions)

1,400
1,300
1,200
1,100
1,000
900
800
700
600
500

1950 1960 1970 1980 1990 2000 2010
(estimate)

Beijing

CHINA

How We Should Eat
Basic Dietary Sources

Every person needs a certain quantity of calories, proteins, and fats, whose minimum daily amounts have been established by the United Nations (U.N.) following specific guidelines based on the energy and nutritional content of the various types of food. About 10-12% of the overall energy amount should come from protein (with a proper balance between animal and vegetable proteins), 25-30% from fats (with a preference for vegetable sources), and the remaining 55-60% should come from carbohydrates, mainly from complex carbohydrates (starch) rather than simple carbohydrates (sugars). These nutrients are found in meat, milk, eggs, fish, most cereals, fruit, vegetables, vegetable and animal oils, and some fungi such as mushrooms.

Proteins have a very high nutritional value, because they provide amino acids which are vital for our body. Meat and other animal products contain a large quantity of protein, while white flour and other processed foods contain very little. Today, the daily per capita protein and calorie consumption is excessive in developed countries, where it is often accompanied by waste and even leads to food-related diseases. In contrast, consumption of protein and calories is dramatically low in poor countries, where the diet is based mainly on cereals.

Calories
(daily average availability per person – 1997)

- more than 3,600
- 3,400-3,600
- 3,200-3,400
  average value in rich countries
- 3,000-3,200
- 2,800-3,000
- 2,600-2,800
- 2,400-2,600
  average value for a good health
- 2,200-2,400
- 2,000-2,200
  average value in developing countries
- 1,800-2,000
- less than 1,800
- data not available

What an American and an Indian Eat

The diet of people living in a wealthy country such as the United States is varied and abundant. It is typically rich in meat, sugars, and animal fats, but poor in whole grain cereals and beans. In a country such as India, however, meals often consist of a simple dish of rice with vegetables and bread. Meat consumption is very limited in India, in part because of the Hindu ban on beef, widespread vegetarianism, the Muslim ban on pork, and rules about specific slaughtering methods. Recent market globalization, however, has led to increased internationalization of foods, so that it is not difficult to find typical Western fast foods in India too.

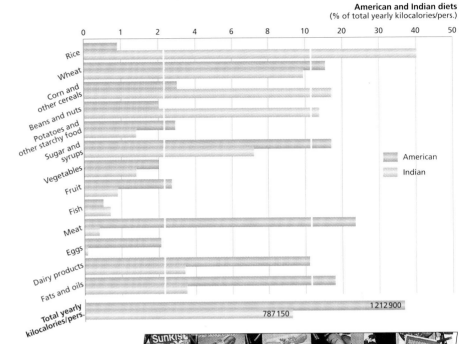

American and Indian diets
(% of total yearly kilocalories/pers.)

Rice, Wheat, Corn and other cereals, Beans and nuts, Potatoes and other starchy food, Sugar and syrups, Vegetables, Fruit, Fish, Meat, Eggs, Dairy products, Fats and oils

American / Indian

Total yearly kilocalories/pers.: 1 212 900 / 787 150

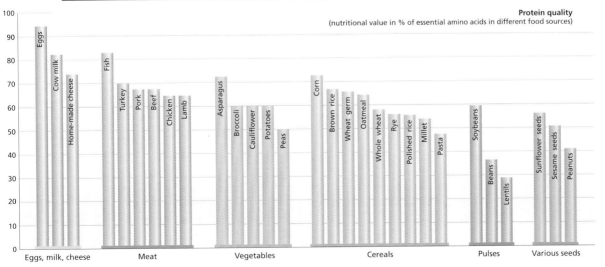

Protein quality
(nutritional value in % of essential amino acids in different food sources)

Eggs, milk, cheese: Eggs, Cow milk, Home-made cheese

Meat: Fish, Turkey, Pork, Beef, Chicken, Lamb

Vegetables: Asparagus, Broccoli, Cauliflower, Potatoes, Peas

Cereals: Corn, Brown rice, Wheat germ, Oatmeal, Whole wheat, Rye, Polished rice, Millet, Pasta

Pulses: Soybeans, Beans, Lentils

Various seeds: Sunflower seeds, Sesame seeds, Peanuts

Not only is food different in various countries, but the ways of cooking and eating differ too. Africans enjoy fruit, manioc, and cultivated corn; the Asian staple is rice. Some products, like Coca Cola, are found everywhere in the world. Whether eating with cutlery, chopsticks, or hands, most people have the majority of their meals at home, although Westerners increasingly eat at restaurants, school, or work.

Food as a Resource
Food and Nutrition

Access to food is universally recognized as a fundamental human right. Food resources, however, are distributed unevenly across the planet, and the agricultural policies pursued by rich and poor countries often create hunger and food insecurity.

Today, more than 800 million people lack adequate food, although food production over the last 35 years has increased more rapidly than the population. It is estimated that every human being would enjoy 2,760 calories per day—more than enough to lead a healthy life—if all the world's food resources were distributed evenly among the world's population. Instead, food is abundant or excessive in developed countries, where population increase is slow and where technical progress allows for constant increases in food production. At the same time, food supplies remain inadequate, from both a quantitative and qualitative standpoint, in

underdeveloped countries, where population growth is rapid and agricultural development is difficult because of obsolete techniques, lack of funds, and the existing agricultural system. Food distribution itself remains a critical problem, especially to remote areas suffering from famine due to drought, war, and other causes.

Extraordinary subsidies granted by wealthy countries are not enough. There is some promise of improvement with new approaches, such as the "green revolutions" already begun in India and Pakistan. These aim at extending farmland and increasing the yield of existing lands, introducing new varieties of cereals, using fertilizers and parasiticides (with caution because of their toxicity), improving irrigation, and applying biotechnologies to food production. Fish farming may also compensate for the continuing drop in the world catch of fish.

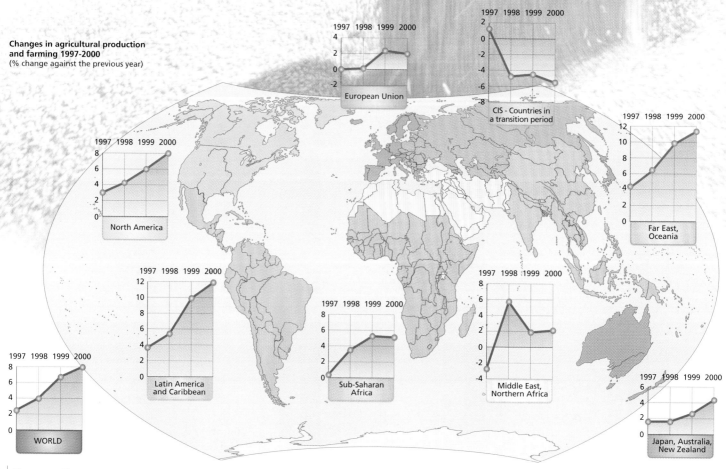

Changes in agricultural production and farming 1997-2000
(% change against the previous year)

Main food plants
(millions of tons - 1999)

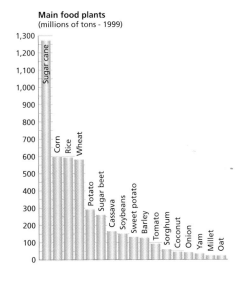

Sugar cane, Corn, Rice, Wheat, Potato, Sugar beet, Cassava, Soybeans, Sweet potato, Barley, Tomato, Sorghum, Coconut, Onion, Yam, Millet, Oat

World fish catch
(millions of tons)

Marine Aquaculture · Marine catch · Inland water catch · Inland waters aquaculture · **Fish availability** *(kg per person)*

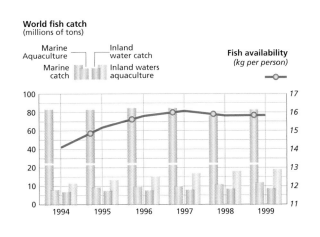

1994 1995 1996 1997 1998 1999

Main meat-producing animals
(millions of tons - 1999)

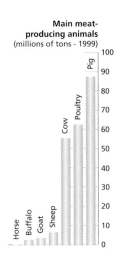

Horse, Buffalo, Goat, Sheep, Cow, Poultry, Pig

focusON

Dependence on Exports

In many countries of Asia, Africa, and Latin America, plantation agriculture is very widespread and mainly focuses on monocultures of one or more types of produce for exports, such as natural rubber, cotton, cocoa, sugar cane, coffee, tea, peanuts, or bananas. Some of these types of produce were introduced in the 16th century following the first colonial conquests by the Europeans. Some, such as peanuts in Senegal and sugar cane in Brazil, were totally unknown to the local population. Planted on the landed estates and controlled by local owners or by foreign multinational companies, the plantations cover the best lands, but do not produce widespread wealth and do not provide the population with the food it needs for a balanced diet. Consequently, agricultural powers like Brazil are experiencing a heavy food deficit in spite of extensive farming.

Dependence on exports
(% of total exports for some Sub-Saharan African countries)

Cocoa		Coffee		Cotton		Tea	
Côte d'Ivoire	30	Burundi	70	Benin	38	Burundi	8
Ghana	24	Central African R.	22	Burkina Faso	39	Rwanda	12
São Tomé and Príncipe	44	Côte d'Ivoire	9	Central African Rep.	46	Tanzania	2
		Ethiopia	8	Chad	12		
		Madagascar	60	Côte d'Ivoire	42		
		Rwanda	45	Mali	3		
		Tanzania	56	Sudan	18		
		Uganda	11	Tanzania	20		
				Togo	3		
				Uganda	10		

The economies of many countries are heavily dependent on the cultivation and export of one single cash crop. Senegal depends on peanuts; Colombia, El Salvador, Uganda, Tanzania, and Burundi rely on coffee; the Ivory Coast grows cocoa, coffee, and pineapple; and Myanmar exports teak wood.

Health and Social Welfare

One measure of the level of development of a country is the health of its citizens. Mortality and infant mortality rates, life expectancy, and the availability of doctors and hospital beds are very different in developed and developing countries. Indeed, poverty leads to a vicious circle: Insufficient incomes force people to live in bad hygienic conditions and to suffer because of undernourishment. This fosters the spread of diseases that often become endemic and further affect the population's ability to work. Thus their opportunities to improve the situation or pay for local medical clinics and hospitals are reduced. Access to drinking water also plays a crucial role in public health. Contaminated water spreads infectious epidemics, like yellow fever and leptospirosis. Stagnant waters host mosquitoes and larvae, which transmit malaria and schistosomiasis.

The money that a country spends on social programs is another important indicator, since this money is used to help people facing difficulties (day care for working mothers, health care services for the elderly and sick, disability pensions, unemployment benefits, and so on) and to take supportive measures for the population as a whole.

The aging of the global population is an unprecedented phenomenon in the history of mankind. Even though it means people are, on average, healthier than ever, it poses several problems. Elderly people need assistance that today's smaller families cannot provide. They need more medical treatments, which means increased health care costs. Of greatest concern, social security systems are disrupted because a decreasing number of workers must support an increasingly large number of pensioners.

Europe and Central Asia

Middle East and Northern Africa

North America

Eastern Asia and the Pacific

Southern Asia

Latin America and Caribbean

Sub-Saharan Africa

Number of people per medical doctor

	Less than 500
	500-1,000
	1,001-2,000
	2,001-5,000
	5,001-10,000
	10,001-20,000
	more than 20,000
	data not available

Hospital beds
(per 10,000 people)
= 1 bed

The AIDS Epidemic in Africa

AIDS keeps spreading across the world, but 70% of the people infected (around 25.3 million) live in sub-Saharan Africa, which also accounts for 80% of the infected children below the age of 15. Since the beginning of the epidemic, one-quarter of the deaths from AIDS has occured in this region. In eight African countries, at least 15% of the adult population is infected. Half the patients contract the virus before the age of 25, and many of them die before they reach the age of 35. In countries like Uganda, Zambia, and Zimbabwe, the disease is killing millions of young people.

South Africa has the highest number of AIDS patients in the world (4.2 million infected) and the fastest growth of the epidemic. Already, one out of four South African women between 20 and 29 years old has contracted the virus, which then may be transmitted from mothers to children during pregnancy. Between 2000 and 2005, life expectancy in seven African countries is expected, by some estimates, to shorten by 17 years because of AIDS: Botswana, Kenya, Lesotho, Namibia, South Africa, Swaziland, and Zimbabwe. In Botswana, between 1995 and 2000, life expectancy was already 23 years shorter than it would have been without AIDS.

The costs of AIDS

Country	Direct cost per patient (in US dollars)	GDP/pers.
Kenya (1992)	938	333
Malawi (1989)	210	203
Rwanda (1989/90)	358	269
Tanzania (1990)	290	204
Zimbabwe (1991)	614	648

Thanks to the UNICEF campaigns, the rate of children vaccinated against six killer diseases (poliomyelitis, measles, pertussis, tetanus, diphtheria, tuberculosis) increased from 5% in 1974 to 74% in 1998. The vaccination programs now save three million children all around the world every year.

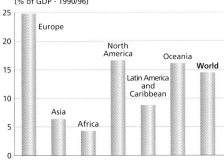

AIDS diffusion
(% of the adult population - 1999)

0.5 1 5 20

☐ data not available

Social security expenditure
(% of GDP - 1990/96)

Welfare systems were first set up in industrial societies. Welfare is partly sustained by taxes and guarantees some types of assistance that (in traditional societies) had formerly been provided by the person's family, social group, village, guild, or associations. In poorer countries, however, the government is often not able to grant such assistance. Voters and politicians decide the scope—and cost to taxpayers—of services, which vary from country to country.

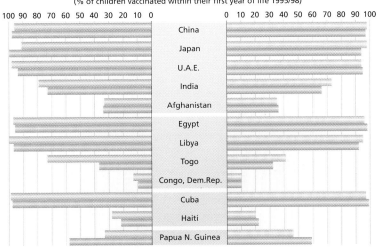

Disease prevention in some countries
(% of children vaccinated within their first year of life 1995/98)

100 90 80 70 60 50 40 30 20 10 0   0 10 20 30 40 50 60 70 80 90 100

China
Japan
U.A.E.
India
Afghanistan
Egypt
Libya
Togo
Congo, Dem.Rep.
Cuba
Haiti
Papua N. Guinea

Tuberculosis
Diphtheria
Poliomyelitis
Measles

Life Expectancy at Birth

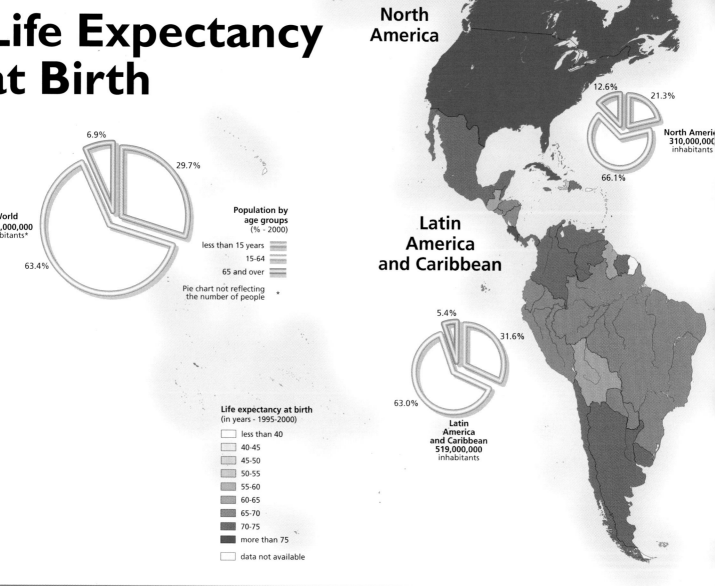

North America

Latin America and Caribbean

6.9%

29.7%

World
6,055,000,000
inhabitants*

63.4%

Population by age groups
(% - 2000)

less than 15 years

15-64

65 and over

Pie chart not reflecting
the number of people *

12.6%   21.3%

North America
310,000,000
inhabitants

66.1%

5.4%

31.6%

63.0%

Latin America and Caribbean
519,000,000
inhabitants

Life expectancy at birth
(in years - 1995-2000)

less than 40

40-45

45-50

50-55

55-60

60-65

65-70

70-75

more than 75

data not available

Variations in life expectancy, in years
(in relation to the periods
1970-1975 and 1995-2000)

more than 20

from 14 to 20

from 9 to 14

from 4 to 9

from 1 to 4

- 2

- 6

below - 6

data not available

Europe

14.7%

17.4%

67.8%

Europe
729,000,000
inhabitants

Asia

5.9%

29.9%

64.2%

Asia
3,683,000,000
inhabitants*

Africa

3.2%

42.5%

54.3%

Africa
784,000,000
inhabitants

Oceania

9.9%

25.3%

64.8%

Oceania
30,400,000
inhabitants

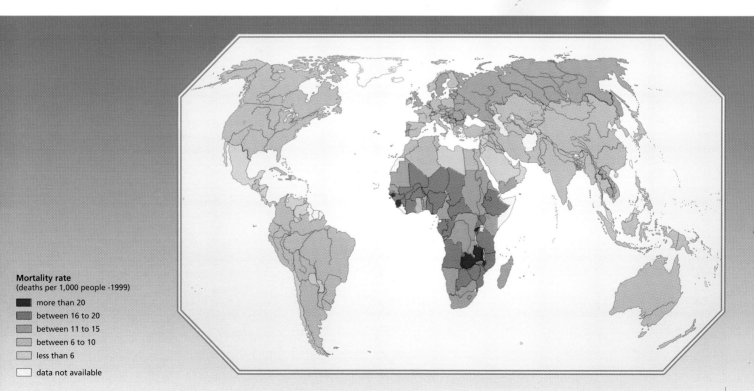

Mortality rate
(deaths per 1,000 people -1999)

- more than 20
- between 16 to 20
- between 11 to 15
- between 6 to 10
- less than 6
- data not available

Health and Survival

The health of a population starts at birth or perhaps even before, if we consider that many diseases, including the terrible AIDS virus, can be transmitted in the mother's womb. The drop in infant mortality (the percentage of children who die in the first year of life over the total number of children born alive) is the first health objective pursued by all countries. This heavily depends on hygienic-environmental factors such as diet, tests taken during pregnancy, assistance during delivery, the protection of mothers, and vaccinations. Some 30,500 children die every day in the world because of common diseases, most of which could be eliminated through vaccination.

Over the last century, infant mortality and mortality below the age of five continued to drop. At the beginning of the new millennium, though, AIDS, wars, and extreme poverty are wiping out the good results achieved, and in some countries they are causing utter devastation. Even in rich countries, the poorest population groups are afflicted by malnutrition and diseases. In Great Britain and in Italy, for instance, almost one-quarter of the children live in poor families. Finally, according to the United Nations, about 5,500 children die every day because of environmental degradation.

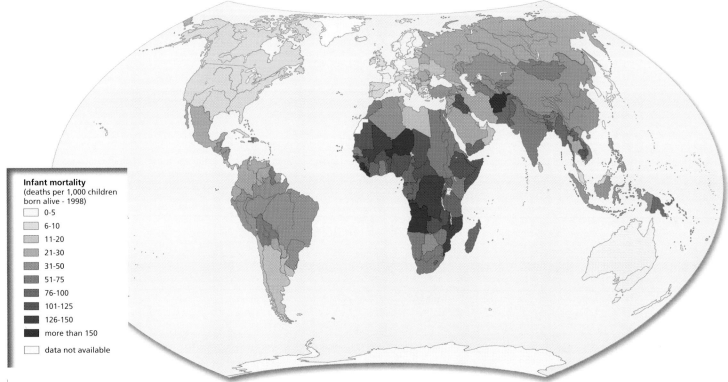

Infant mortality
(deaths per 1,000 children born alive - 1998)

- 0-5
- 6-10
- 11-20
- 21-30
- 31-50
- 51-75
- 76-100
- 101-125
- 126-150
- more than 150
- data not available

Aid in Favor of Childhood

Half of the world's poor, some 600 million people, are children. Today, in 80 countries, the per capita income is lower than a decade ago; but aid for development keeps decreasing. From 1992 to 1997, aid dropped by 21% worldwide, and by over 33% in the main industrialized countries.

International aid is considered vital to overcome emergency situations (wars, famines, natural disasters), among whose victims children are the weakest. In the last ten years, wars have killed over two million children, and six million have been injured and maimed, while more than 300,000 have been recruited as little soldiers.

Financial aid can be extremely useful, sometimes decisive, even in "normal" conditions. For example, on average, 20 U.S. dollars are enough to vaccinate a child against the six most common diseases.

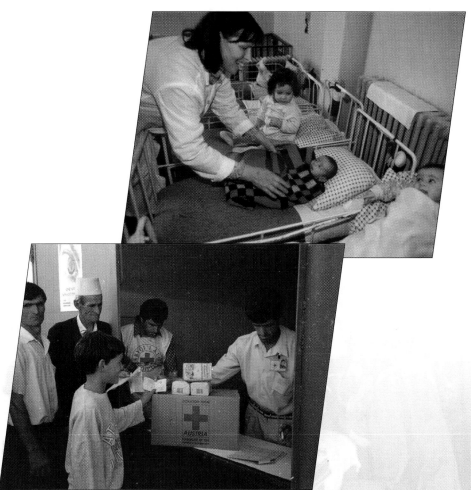

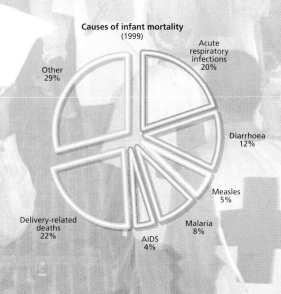

More than 500,000 women die every year from causes related to delivery or pregnancy, and over 99% of these deaths take place in developing countries. These data are tragic and meaningful: A woman giving birth to her child in sub-Saharan Africa has a one in 13 chance of dying due to a total absence of basic health and prenatal care. In industrialized countries this risk drops to a one in 4,100 chance.

Causes of infant mortality
(1999)

- Other 29%
- Acute respiratory infections 20%
- Diarrhoea 12%
- Measles 5%
- Malaria 8%
- AIDS 4%
- Delivery-related deaths 22%

Maternal delivery-related mortality
(number of deaths per 100,000 deliveries)

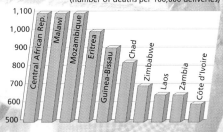

Central African Rep., Malawi, Mozambique, Eritrea, Guinea-Bissau, Chad, Zimbabwe, Laos, Zambia, Côte d'Ivoire

Infant mortality
(deaths per 1,000 children before the age of 5)

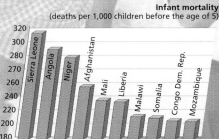

Sierra Leone, Angola, Niger, Afghanistan, Mali, Liberia, Malawi, Somalia, Congo Dem. Rep., Mozambique

Main causes of death (1985-1997)	Developing countries		Developed countries	
	1985	1997	1985	1997
Infections and parasite diseases	45%	43%	5%	1%
Cardio-vascular conditions	16%	24%	51%	46%
Delivery	10%	10%	1%	1%
Cancer	6%	9%	21%	21%
Respiratory system conditions	6%	5%	4%	8%
Other or unknown causes	17%	9%	18%	23%
Total deaths	37,000,000	40,000,000	11,000,000	12,000,000

School Enrollment

Access to education is one of humanity's fundamental rights because of its immense power to transform the individual, improve society, and foster social progress. This right, however, is far from being granted in all countries, especially in those where there are wars, intolerance, natural disasters, and hunger. The average level of education that a population reaches is a very complex phenomenon. Economic, social, cultural, and political aspects combine and lead to a figure—nearly one billion adult illiterates—that, on a global scale, mainly involves the least developed countries and, from a social viewpoint, the poorest social classes.

In the last few decades, school enrollment rates have increased considerably, particularly in Latin America and in Asia. However, much still needs to be done in order to ensure that everyone gets primary education. The next goals are increased enrollment in secondary education, and improved quality of teaching. It is also necessary for schools to reach the underprivileged, including girls, children living in rural areas, and those belonging to ethnic and linguistic minorities, as well as the disabled, and children involved in wars or other emergency situations.

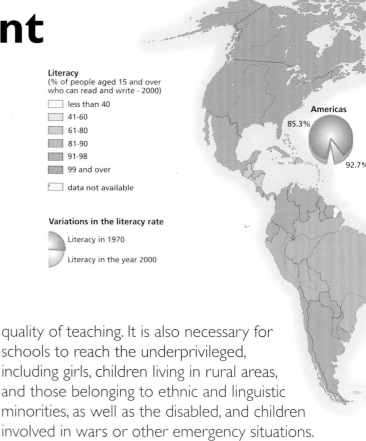

Literacy
(% of people aged 15 and over who can read and write - 2000)

- [ ] less than 40
- [ ] 41-60
- [ ] 61-80
- [ ] 81-90
- [ ] 91-98
- [ ] 99 and over
- [ ] data not available

Variations in the literacy rate

Literacy in 1970

Literacy in the year 2000

Americas
85.3%
92.7%

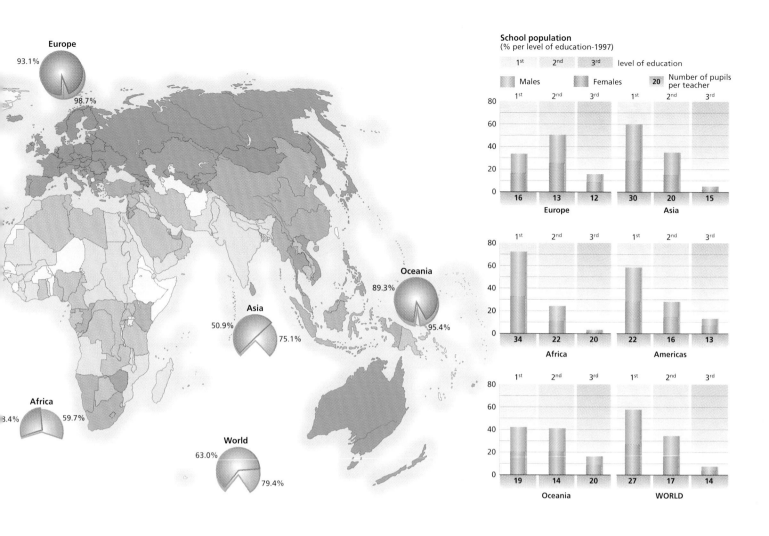

School population
(% per level of education-1997)

| 1st | 2nd | 3rd | level of education |

| Males | Females | 20 | Number of pupils per teacher |

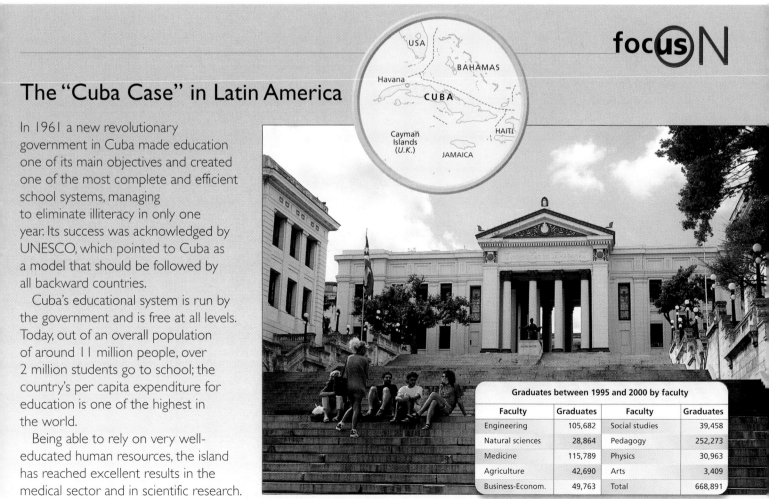

The "Cuba Case" in Latin America

focus**O**N

In 1961 a new revolutionary government in Cuba made education one of its main objectives and created one of the most complete and efficient school systems, managing to eliminate illiteracy in only one year. Its success was acknowledged by UNESCO, which pointed to Cuba as a model that should be followed by all backward countries.

Cuba's educational system is run by the government and is free at all levels. Today, out of an overall population of around 11 million people, over 2 million students go to school; the country's per capita expenditure for education is one of the highest in the world.

Being able to rely on very well-educated human resources, the island has reached excellent results in the medical sector and in scientific research.

Graduates between 1995 and 2000 by faculty

Faculty	Graduates	Faculty	Graduates
Engineering	105,682	Social studies	39,458
Natural sciences	28,864	Pedagogy	252,273
Medicine	115,789	Physics	30,963
Agriculture	42,690	Arts	3,409
Business-Econom.	49,763	Total	668,891

Women's Education

People's need to tackle problems of simple survival before dealing with education has led to a dramatic situation: 86 million girls across the world do not receive any primary education. As a result, and for a variety of cultural reasons, two-thirds of the world's one billion illiterate adults are women.

Although women are the overwhelming majority of the illiterate, the importance of female education is universally recognized, because it deeply influences the strength of a society. Educated women's children tend to be better nourished, fall ill less frequently, and, in turn, are sent to school themselves. Indeed, educated women in general get married later, have fewer children, devote themselves to improving their family's situation, take part in political and economic decisions, and are active in their communities.

The problem of illiteracy is dramatic in Southeast Asia, in Africa, and in the Arab world, where more than half the women cannot read or write. In these countries, girls leave school two years before boys and eight years before women in industrialized countries. Girls in the United States, France, and Canada study on average for twelve years. Female students in countries such as Burkina Faso and Afghanistan attend school for a much shorter period of time.

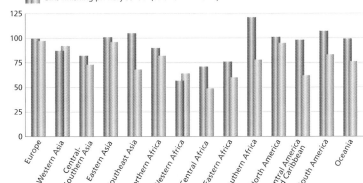

Percentage of girls enrolling in and finishing primary school

▮ Enrollments (% of the total number of girls from the related age bracket*)
▮ Girls finishing primary school (% of enrollments)

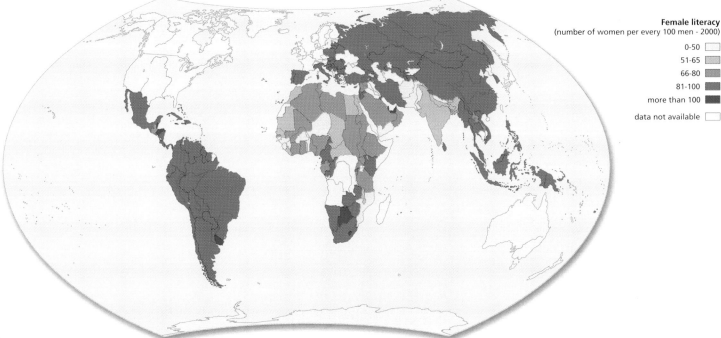

Female literacy
(number of women per every 100 men - 2000)

0-50
51-65
66-80
81-100
more than 100
data not available

focus⊙N

Graduated Women

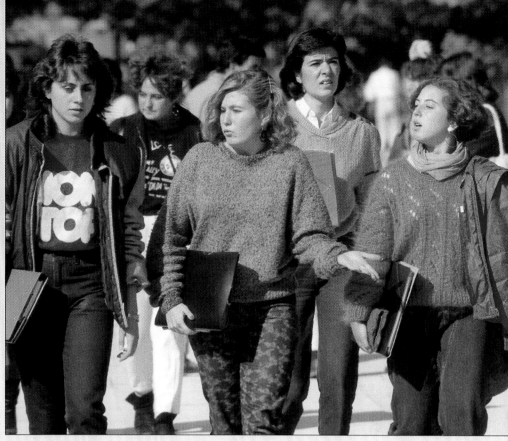

Women gained access to higher education very recently. Until the first half of the 1900s, the percentage of women holding a university degree or a graduation certificate was extremely low. In America and Europe, no woman graduated before 1867. In England, women were not allowed to enroll at the University of Cambridge until 1948. In some nations, the posts of dean or headmaster were barred to women until the 1950s. The Nobel Prize, first awarded in 1901, has been given to only ten female scientists in the past century. Although they had taken part in projects which were awarded the Nobel Prize, outstanding researchers such as the molecular biologist Rosalind Franklin, the astronomer Jocelyn Bell-Burnell, and the physicists Lise Meitner and Chien-Shiung Wu had to step back in favor of their male colleagues.

The role played by women in the world of knowledge is heavily influenced by cultural and religious traditions around the world that, until women organized their struggle to get the vote in the late 1800s and early 1900s, prevented them from full rights as citizens, and typically limited them to the house-bound roles of wife and mother.

In the last few decades, the presence of women in higher education has made considerable progress: in some countries the number of women equals or is higher than the number of men. However, real equality has been reached only in developed countries, at the primary and secondary school level. Female enrollment at universities is still lower than male enrollment, and female presence is particularly smaller on technical and scientific faculties.

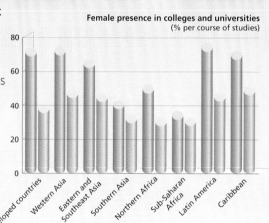

Female presence in colleges and universities
(% per course of studies)

Developed countries · Western Asia · Eastern and Southeast Asia · Southern Asia · Northern Africa · Sub-Saharan Africa · Latin America · Caribbean

◯ Faculties of cultural studies ◯ Scientific faculties

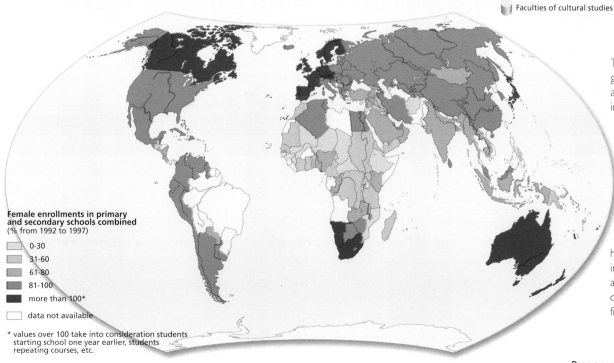

Female enrollments in primary and secondary schools combined
(% from 1992 to 1997)

- 0-30
- 31-60
- 61-80
- 81-100
- more than 100*
- data not available

* values over 100 take into consideration students starting school one year earlier, students repeating courses, etc.

The school enrollment gap between males and females increases in secondary schools and universities, even in some developed countries. Indeed, if the cost of education heavily affects the family budget, male children are favored. If the family needs help or an additional income, it is girls who are usually told to help out and are prevented from going to school.

The Work Force
Economic Sectors and Education

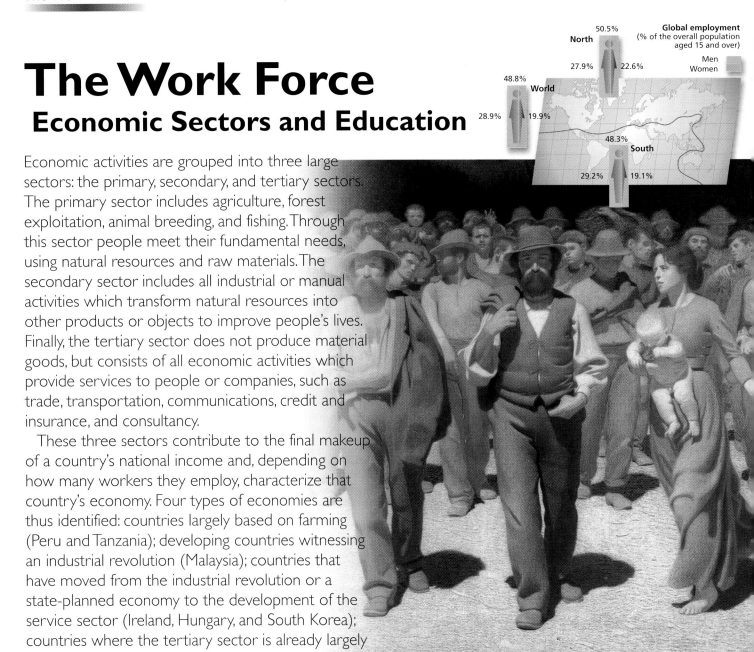

Global employment
(% of the overall population
aged 15 and over)

Men
Women

North 50.5%

27.9%   22.6%

World 48.8%

28.9%   19.9%

South 48.3%

29.2%   19.1%

Economic activities are grouped into three large sectors: the primary, secondary, and tertiary sectors. The primary sector includes agriculture, forest exploitation, animal breeding, and fishing. Through this sector people meet their fundamental needs, using natural resources and raw materials. The secondary sector includes all industrial or manual activities which transform natural resources into other products or objects to improve people's lives. Finally, the tertiary sector does not produce material goods, but consists of all economic activities which provide services to people or companies, such as trade, transportation, communications, credit and insurance, and consultancy.

These three sectors contribute to the final makeup of a country's national income and, depending on how many workers they employ, characterize that country's economy. Four types of economies are thus identified: countries largely based on farming (Peru and Tanzania); developing countries witnessing an industrial revolution (Malaysia); countries that have moved from the industrial revolution or a state-planned economy to the development of the service sector (Ireland, Hungary, and South Korea); countries where the tertiary sector is already largely established (many Western economies).

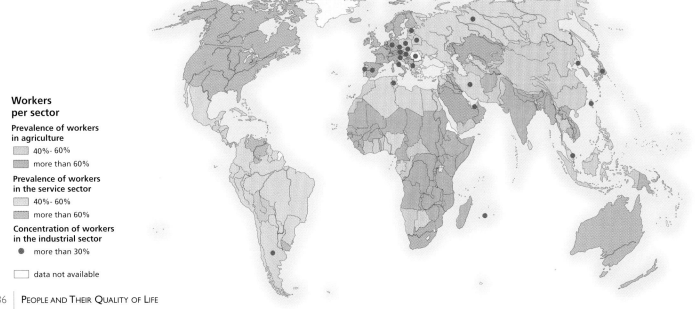

**Workers
per sector**

**Prevalence of workers
in agriculture**

- 40%- 60%
- more than 60%

**Prevalence of workers
in the service sector**

- 40%- 60%
- more than 60%

**Concentration of workers
in the industrial sector**

- more than 30%

- data not available

Juvenile unemployment
(% of young people between 15 and 24 years)

- less than 10
- 10 - 20
- 20 - 30
- 30 - 40
- more than 40
- data not available

One-third of the world's work force, nearly one billion people, is unemployed or underemployed. The situation is particularly alarming among young people. There are about 70 million youngsters unemployed and there are many more working in miserable conditions, often illegally. In many African and Asian countries, those between the ages of 15 and 24 account for 50% of the total number of unemployed. Consequently, young people—who represent the main human resource of the countries traveling the path of economic development, social progress, and technological innovation—are often afflicted with uncertainty about their future and are not given the opportunity to participate meaningfully in the work force. This often leads to increased social problems and crime.

In almost all countries, a high level of education improves opportunities to find a job. Now, computer illiteracy adds to the gap in skills between those with and without higher education. Policies promoting educaton in the new technologies are required in order to avoid the social problems that come with underemployment and unemployment.

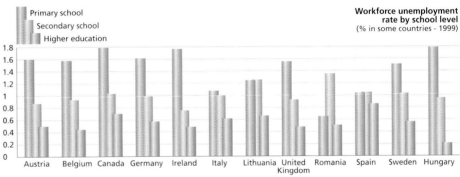

- Primary school
- Secondary school
- Higher education

Workforce unemployment rate by school level
(% in some countries - 1999)

Austria, Belgium, Canada, Germany, Ireland, Italy, Lithuania, United Kingdom, Romania, Spain, Sweden, Hungary

The workload
(number of hours worked per year per person)

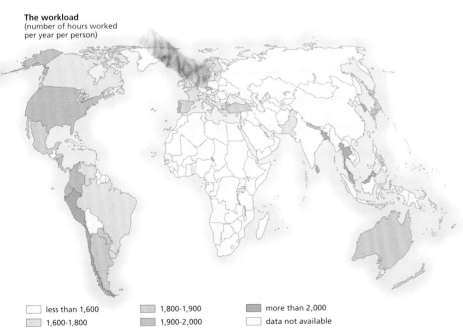

- less than 1,600
- 1,600-1,800
- 1,800-1,900
- 1,900-2,000
- more than 2,000
- data not available

Limits on the number of working hours (ensuring the workers' right to adequate rest) has been the objective of union struggles all over the world and is now a right safeguarded in almost all countries.

Women and Work

Women today represent an increasing percentage of the global work force. Moving beyond the cultural traditions that kept them at home (and tied to the responsibilities of child rearing) for most of human history, women now comprise over a third of the world's workers. Their global work force participation rate is 43% of all women, compared to a rate of 73% for men. Women's participation ranges from 60% in industrialized countries to about 10% in North Africa and Western Asia. These statistics fail, however, to show the total picture, since much "women's work" (housework, childcare, working in the fields, water and wood collection) is not counted.

Women are generally paid less than men. For example, in the European textile, clothing, and footware industries, men are paid some 20-30% more than women. When competing with men, women often face discrimination and endure poorer working conditions. Self-employment, part-time jobs, and home-based work have increased women's opportunities, but are usually poorly paid and lack social benefits.

For years, women have been employed in heavy industry, where they perform the same tasks and work the same hours as men, but where they are often discriminated against in terms of wages and promotion. Women migrant workers and those living in the countryside tend to suffer social exclusion, have fewer job opportunities, are more likely to lose their job than men, and are more vulnerable to abuse and sexual harrassment than male workers.

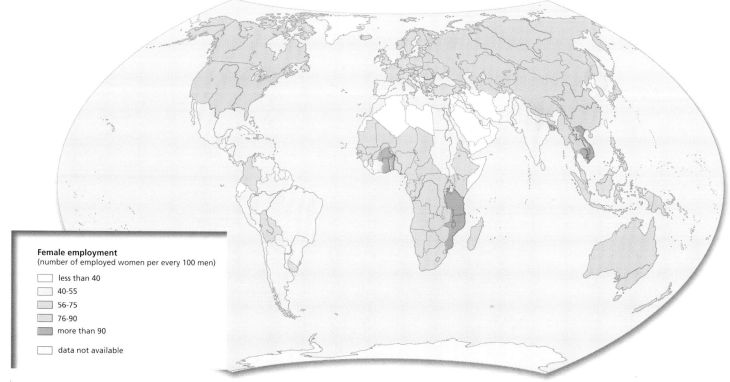

Female employment
(number of employed women per every 100 men)

- less than 40
- 40-55
- 56-75
- 76-90
- more than 90

- data not available

Working Women

The right to vote, own property, receive equal education, and work outside the home are relatively new rights for women, only truly established in the last century. Women must still struggle with discrimination that has made them second class citizens for most of human history. Following an increase in the level of women's education, today many women hold positions of responsibility, including entrepreneurs, ministers, senior Army officers, managers, freelancers, professors, and scientists. Nonetheless, the UN's International Labor Organization (ILO) highlights that gender equality is still far from being attained. Most women workers still have traditional, low-paying jobs: secretary,

cashier, switchboard operator, teacher, shop assistant, nurse, and other non-managerial positions. But even when holding the same professional position as men, and in countries where women equal men in terms of finding a job after graduation, women generally earn 20-30% less than men do.

In terms of political power, women remain heavily underrepresented in governments, political parties, and even at the United Nations. Consequently, they are less able to make their voice heard, highlight their problems, and influence important decisions which have a bearing on their quality of life and on society as a whole.

Women's leadership
- **Representation at the UN:** **7** women in 1994, **12** in 2000
- **Governments: 14** women holding the post of Prime Minister or Head of State. **12%** in national parliaments
- **Company Executives: 11-12%** of the executives in the 500 main industries in the US and Canada, but only **3%** at the highest levels; **7%** of the executives in the first 5,000 French companies
- **New Companies:** In developed countries women have established **twice** as many companies as men have.
- **www: 47%** of women, compared to 41% of men, use the Internet and on-line services for their work. **23%** set up an Internet site for their company compared to 16% of men.

Women managers
(% of female staff on the overall executive staff)
- 0-10
- 11-30
- 31-50
- more than 50

Female work
(index value as a % of male work in some countries)

In many countries the law recognizes and safeguards the vital role played by women as mothers. This, however, is far from relieving women of the burden of housework and caring for the family (including the elderly), tasks that fall almost entirely on women and often represent a second "job".

Children at Work
Childhood Denied

Child labor is widespread all over the world. Unfortunately, hundreds of millions of children have to work, instead of going to school. Half of them work ten hours a day or longer. They drag rocks in stone quarries, they scavenge through waste, weave carpets, knead clay into bricks, sell goods at traffic lights, manufacture balls and shoes, wash cars, work in the fields, and even beg or prostitute themselves on the street.

Child labor is often dangerous and always hard. It is a direct consequence of poverty, but it also prevents children from escaping the misery of poverty, since children who cannot go to school will not become qualified workers.

Children are preferred to adult workers in many cases because of their docility, their manual skills, and, particularly, because they can be paid low wages. Child exploitation often borders on slavery. Children generally work for low or no wages for a high number of working hours, have no right to leave the job, are often mistreated and abused, and, in many cases, must hand over their earnings to pay for the debts created by their parents.

It is in poorer or developing countries that natural disasters, economic and political instability, AIDS, migrations, and wars force a growing number of children to take on heavy (and sometimes illegal) jobs. In 2001, 22 developed countries ratified a proposal (Convention 182) aimed at stopping child exploitation in 90 countries, by promoting development and education, and calling for child protection laws.

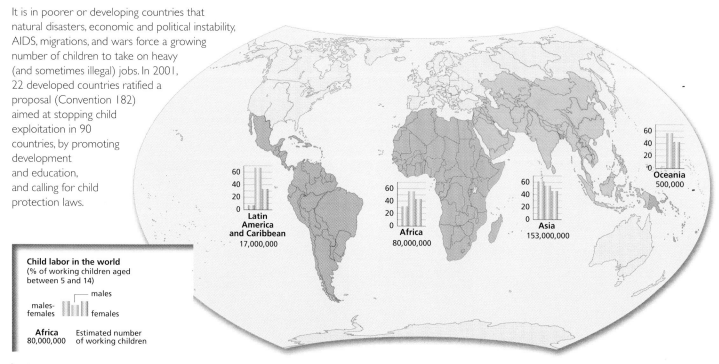

Latin America and Caribbean
17,000,000

Africa
80,000,000

Asia
153,000,000

Oceania
500,000

Child labor in the world
(% of working children aged between 5 and 14)

males-females

males

females

Africa
80,000,000

Estimated number of working children

Statistics Reveal a Hidden Tragedy

It is difficult to calculate the exact extent of child labor, because it is defined differently in various countries, and also because it is often illegal. Until a few years ago, statistics took into consideration only children over the age of ten, while in some countries children under age ten account for 20% of child labor in the countryside and 5% in urban areas. Moreover, girls were not accounted for, nor were teenagers working full time doing housework.

International childhood organizations, therefore, had to adopt new statistical methods. More reliable estimates, for instance, are achieved by taking into account those children who, although still falling within the compulsory school age bracket, do not go to school. The results highlight a tragedy which goes far beyond any expectation—hundreds of millions of children between five and 14 years old work all over the world. This occurs not only in poor or developing countries: 2.5 million children are reportedly forced to work in industrialized countries, and 2.4 million in countries with a transitional economy, particularly in Asia and Eastern Europe. In these countries, the majority of children (70%) work in the agricultural and fishing sectors, 8% in the manufacturing and trade sectors, and 7%, especially girls, are engaged in housework within their own family or for other families. The remaining child workers toil in the building sector, transportation, or mines, or simply scavange and beg to survive.

The dimensions of an age-old tragedy that continues in our time

- **250 million** children between ages 5 and 17 are forced to work, **110 million** of whom are girls
- **179 million** have jobs dangerous for their physical, mental or moral health
- **111 million** children under the age of 15 and **59 million** young people between 15 and 17 are forced into dangerous jobs
- **8.4 million** children are subjected to: slavery, slavery related to debts, forced army recruitment, prostitution, pornography, drug dealing and other illegal activities
- **14-17%** of the world's children who do not attend school work more than 49 hours per week
- **11-13%** of the world's children work more than 56 hours per week

---

Child labor often takes on huge proportions in the mining industry and in commercial agriculture related to the world markets. Surveys carried out in Brazil, Kenya, and Mexico show that in these sectors 25-30% of the work force consists of children who have not reached the age of 15. In the countryside, children—particularly girls—tend to start working very early, between five and seven years old.

With the rapidly increasing urbanization which characterizes developing countries, the number of children working in the trade sector, in restaurants and hotels, in handicraft workshops, and in small industries is increasing at a fast rate.

Culture and Information
The Importance of the Press

The press is a powerful medium because it is able to cheaply reproduce enormous numbers of copies of text, in order to reach an equally large number of people. In spite of competition by new technologies, such as the computer and satellite-based World Wide Web, the press has not lost its vital ability to disseminate news and help form public opinion. If newspapers have survived almost 100 years of radio and over 50 years of television news, it is in part because written text allows for more in-depth comments and reflection than is usually provided by radio or television.

Today, over 8,000 daily newspapers are published in the world and are read by around two billion people. The maximum circulations are found in industrialized countries, headed by Japan and Eastern Europe, followed by North America, Australia, and Western Europe. In developing countries, the number of published newspapers is considerably lower, mainly due to higher illiteracy and lower incomes. The spread of the press is also affected, however, by many other historical and cultural factors. For instance, where various languages are

spoken or numerous ethnic groups live together, as in Canada or Switzerland, many daily newspapers are published, representing a variety of cultural groups. In countries which have high national cohesion, like France or Great Britain, conversely, fewer papers are published, but higher numbers of copies are printed. The number of published books is increasing rapidly too. The United States is the leader in this sector, with Western Europe and Japan, which together publish 61% of all the world's books.

Dailies published
(daily circulation per 1,000 people - 1996)

102   187

100
80
60
40
20
0

Europe and Central Asia | Northern Africa and the Middle-East | Sub-Saharan Africa | North America | Latin America and Caribbean

Dailies
(daily circulation per 1,000 people - 1996)

- less than 10
- 10-50
- 51-100
- 101-200
- 201-300
- more than 300
- data not available

focus ON

Vaults of Knowledge

The first libraries were created starting in the 21st century B.C. in Babylonia, where they housed collections of clay tablets. In Egypt, libraries held papyrus scrolls. Between the 4th and 5th century, the use of parchment replaced papyrus scrolls, creating the first books, which consisted of sets of parchment sheets. However, it was in the Middle Ages that libraries spread to all monasteries and schools. Following the invention of European printing in the 1440s and the consequent rapid increase in the number of books, modern libraries were created. In England, the Bodleian Library at Oxford was created in 1602, while the Cambridge Library was founded in 1646. In 1732, the concept of public libraries was established by Benjamin Franklin in the United States, although Boston claims one as early as 1653. In 1800, the American Library of Congress was established. One of the richest and most modern in the world, it has over 75 million items, including almost four million maps. The Lenin Library in Moscow, Russia, counts 30 million books. While the main objective is still to house and share printed materials, public libraries also provide many public services. They house audio recordings, photos, compact discs, microfilm, and also organize cultural events, exhibitions, and conferences.

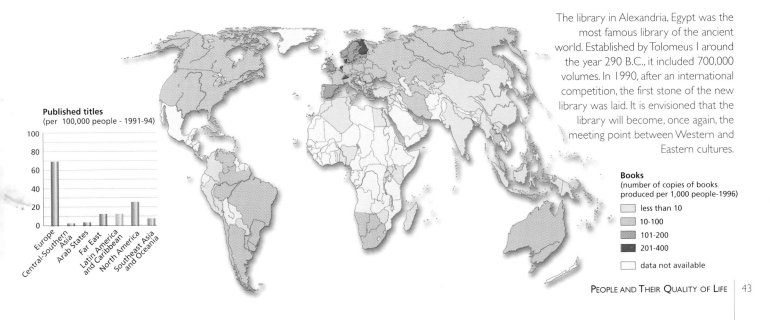

The library in Alexandria, Egypt was the most famous library of the ancient world. Established by Tolomeus I around the year 290 B.C., it included 700,000 volumes. In 1990, after an international competition, the first stone of the new library was laid. It is envisioned that the library will become, once again, the meeting point between Western and Eastern cultures.

Published titles
(per 100,000 people - 1991-94)

100
80
60
40
20
0

Europe
Central-Southern Asia
Arab States
Far East
Latin America and Caribbean
North America
Southeast Asia and Oceania

Books
(number of copies of books produced per 1,000 people-1996)

- less than 10
- 10-100
- 101-200
- 201-400
- data not available

Radio, Television, and Movies
Sounds and Images

Radio and television are media that do not require literacy. Using sound and images, these media communicate in ways that are universally understood. Moreover—especially since television has used satellite transmission—radio and TV are the fastest media, able to broadcast any event at virtually the same time and rate that it is happening. Radio and television are able to disseminate information and culture over any distance, allowing direct communication between all regions of the world. This has created the foundation of a sort of "global village," as it was optimistically defined by the Canadian sociologist Herbert Marshall McLuhan. He saw these media as ways to bring the human family together. American dominance of both the movie and television industries, however, often causes concern in countries wishing to restrict American cultural influence and preserve their own culture.

Nevertheless, international communication—and the "global village" it promotes—are facts of life today. According to UNESCO, radios are very widespread, with on average 418 radios per every 1,000 people in the world. Industrialized countries count more than one radio per person, but it is in developing or poor countries that the radio often

plays its most vital social role. In countries where population is scattered across vast territories, a radio becomes a precious source of information and civic education.

The distribution of television sets mainly involves the wealthier regions of the planet, as well as Latin America and the Middle East. Since television sets are much more expensive than radios, low incomes restrict the poor from access to television. Uneven development of electric networks outside urban areas continues to limit many regions, but satellite and cable television are improving access worldwide.

Radio and television
(number of sets every 1,000 people in some countries)

Country	Radio	TV	Country	Radio	TV
USA	2,146	847	Russia	420	418
Iceland	950	356	China	335	321
Germany	948	580	Iran	280	76
Bolivia	676	116	Chad	236	2
Jamaica	476	182	Vietnam	107	47

The adoption of transistors and integrated circuits allowed for the production of small-size and portable sets which, together with the low production costs in Japan and other Asian countries, led to the spreading of radio to all corners of the planet.
In order to prevent total dependence on Japanese imports, especially for televisions, several countries, like China and Russia, developed their own electronic industry.

North America

Europe and Central Asia

Middle East and Northern Africa

Far East and the Pacific

Southern Asia

Sub-Saharan Africa

Latin America and Caribbean

Televisions
(no. of sets per 1,000 people - 1998)

20

Radios
(no. - of sets per 1,000 people - 1997)

less than 50
50-250
250-500
500-750
750-1,000
more than 1,000
data not available

CNN A Global TV Network

The Cable News Network (CNN) is a TV news station based in Atlanta, Georgia. Founded by Ted Turner in 1980, it was orignally part of his TBS (Turner Broadcasting System) group. Now owned by Time Warner Inc., its programs are devoted to nonstop information and are received via satellite globally except for Siberia and the North and South Poles.

CNN rose to fame during the Gulf War (1991), when its reports, often exclusive and coming direct from the war zone, were broadcast by TV news in all countries. CNN's programs are updated 24 hours a day and involve over 4,000 people, including technicians, journalists, and correspondents placed throughout the world. CNN also features an international edition of its programs (CNN International), and

versions in foreign languages. Its worldwide coverage makes CNN a global network and a precious source of information for the entire world, but it also promotes its own Western cultural viewpoint.

> **CNN data**
> - Satellites used: **17**
> - Broadcasting hours per day: **24**
> - Countries reached by its signal: **212**
> - Viewers in the world: around **1 billion**
> - Viewers in the U.S.: around **86 million**
> - Languages in which it broadcasts: English, Spanish, Turkish, Portuguese, German, Norwegian, Italian, and Swedish

Movies: The Dream Factory

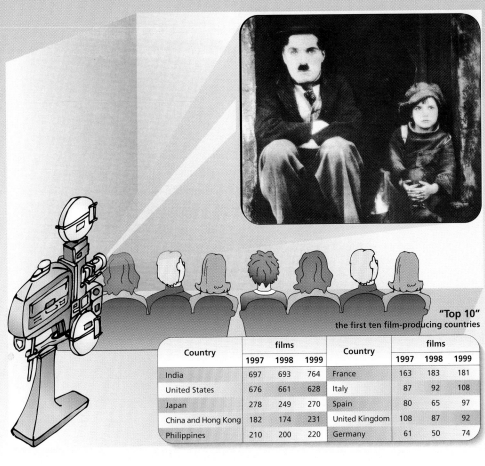

In 1913, the first important American film was shot (*The Squaw Man*) in Hollywood, the Los Angeles suburb which, between the two world wars, would become the "Movie Capital of the World," the international capital of the dream factory. Since then, while film-making requires considerable funds, large markets, and entails considerable risk, the California movie studios have been funded well enough to dominate the export market. Beginning in the early 1990s, however, the world leader in the number of films produced has been India and its movie capital "Bollywood," as Mumbai (formerly Bombay) is often called. With around 800 films per year, Indian cinema is seen by an average of 12.5 million people a day. Primarily geared to the local culture, most of these films are not exported to the West. Nonetheless, Bollywood distributes its films to as many as 80 Asian and African countries.

"Top 10"
the first ten film-producing countries

Country	films			Country	films		
	1997	1998	1999		1997	1998	1999
India	697	693	764	France	163	183	181
United States	676	661	628	Italy	87	92	108
Japan	278	249	270	Spain	80	65	97
China and Hong Kong	182	174	231	United Kingdom	108	87	92
Philippines	210	200	220	Germany	61	50	74

A Traveling World
Tourist Flows and International Tourism

After World War II, the development of the industrial world increased not only salaries, but people's spare time and the use of cars and airplanes. Tourism became a mass phenomenon, feeding a constantly-growing industry, which in the next few decades may become the largest economic activity in the world. Between 1980 and 2000 the tourist industry increased almost fivefold. Half of the tourist travel goes to Europe and one-fourth travels to the Americas, but the most considerable growth has been to the Far East and to Oceania, which, together, grew from 8% (in 1980) to around 20% of the tourist trade in the year 2000. Today, tourist travel generally flows from the north to the south of the world, from industrialized to less

developed countries, in the opposite direction of the migration flows related to work. There are now billions of people traveling every year for tourism: half a billion are "traditional" tourists, another half a billion people travel for business and conference-related tourism. France, the United States, Spain, and Italy are the most visited countries. France records 65 million incoming tourists per year. People coming from the United States, Germany, England, and Japan are the ones spending the most for tourism, followed by the French, the Italians, and the Canadians. These seven groups together spend around 210 billion dollars per year for tourism, a figure equalling the overall gross domestic product of the entire sub-Saharan Africa.

International tourism
(incoming tourists - 1997)
- less than 1 million
- 1-5 million
- 5-10 million
- 10-20 million
- 20-40 million
- more than 40 million
- data not available

"Top 15"
Main tourist destinations
1 million people

Greece, Hong Kong (China), Hungary, Poland, Austria, Germany, Canada, Mexico, Russia, United Kingdom, China, Italy, Spain, United States, France

Looking for Exotic Landscapes, History, and Fun

A huge number of people travel for tourism. What drives them? There are many different motivations: the wish to get away from day-to-day work and city traffic; the desire to enrich one's knowledge; the need to strengthen family or interpersonal relationships; the goal of toning up one's body; spirtitual rejuvenation; and the thirst for adventure.

These are all needs which can be fulfilled in a variety of places and in many different ways. Indeed, today every destination has its appeal, depending on the interests and needs of the tourists.

The main tourist destinations are still the sea and the mountains (for summer holidays and winter sports), together with spas. However, cultural tourism has become very successful too. Its main destinations are cities with art and important events, green tourism, farm stays, school trips, and holidays for the elderly.

The beauty of landscapes and mild climates are secrets of the success enjoyed by exotic places, where the dream of a holiday spent in open spaces can come true, and where whole areas, islands, and archipelagos are entirely devoted to tourists and feature resorts and international clubs. Besides the traditional hotel-based tourism, other approaches have developed as well, ranging from private homes to campsites, from youth hostels to second homes, and—more recently—shared-ownership of vacation houses.

Safaris and cruises are two very successful forms of tourism. The former allow tourists to discover the great African national parks, the latter combine visits to tourist destinations and the comfort of fully-equipped cruise ships, offering many kinds of entertainment.

Europe
361,509,000

Middle East
14,833,000

Africa
23,157,000

Americas
118,481,000

Southern Asia
4,830,000

Far East and the Pacific
87,953,000

Tourist presence
(total arrivals per year
in million people - 1997)

10 50 100 300

main tourist areas

Tourist flows
(total yearly flow
in million people - 1997)
20
10
5

Internal tourist flows
87,953,000

Traveling and Tourism

Tourism often plays a crucial role in the economic expansion of a country. It creates new jobs and is often a powerful way to acquire foreign currency. The balance of payments in some countries directly depends on the currency injection ensured by tourism. However, current world travel, which is increasingly intense, may sometimes irreversibly damage the environment and disrupt the customs, traditions, and ethical-religious cultures of the hosting populations. This is especially true in developing countries. Although sometimes tourism sustains natural ecosystems and safeguards the animal species that attract tourists (as in African parks), it often also destroys exactly what tourists are looking for. In the Caribbean, for example, the tourist demand for seafood is one of the main causes of the diminished numbers of many species, including lobsters.

Tourism revenues often involve only a small elite of the local population. Unfortunately for the hosting countries, in many cases the profits from tourism will eventually leave the country again, as tourist facilities are usually owned by foreign multinational tour operators. The hosting country is often forced to increase the imports of luxury goods and products in order to make tourists happy. This is particularly true in those areas where tourism is the main economic activity, as in the African safari reserves and in those countries where the number of tourists is much higher than the local population, such as on the island of Malta, which welcomes more than one million tourists every year (three times its resident population). Non-Western cultures are the most vulnerable to corruption of their culturual identity, since tourism for pleasure is mainly a product of Western culture.

The sea and the mountains, in one's own country or abroad, are favorite destinations for tourists. Seaside resorts were already popular in the 19th century as places for winter holidays, and then became the favorite summer destination for mass tourism. Mountain valleys were initially loved as health resorts, and then further developed thanks to the spread of sports such as skiing, climbing, and trekking.

Tourism market shares

Arrivals (% of the world total)	**Currency injection** (% of the total value)

Region	Arrivals	Currency injection
Europe	57.7	48.6
Americas	18.5	28.7
Eastern Asia and the Pacific	16	17.3
Africa	4	2.3
Middle East	2.9	2
Southern Asia	0.9	1.1

More tourists than inhabitants
(ratio between the number of tourists and the population)

Country	Tourists	Population	Tourists/inhab. ratio
San Marino	3,264,000	27,000	120
Monaco	259,000	34,000	7.6
Antigua and Barbuda	232,000	68,000	3.4
Malta	1,182,000	380,000	3.1
Cyprus	2,088,000	786,000	2.7
Singapore	6,531,000	3,387,000	1.9
Barbados	472,000	270,000	1.7
Maldives	467,000	269,000	1.7
Seychelles	130,000	77,000	1.7

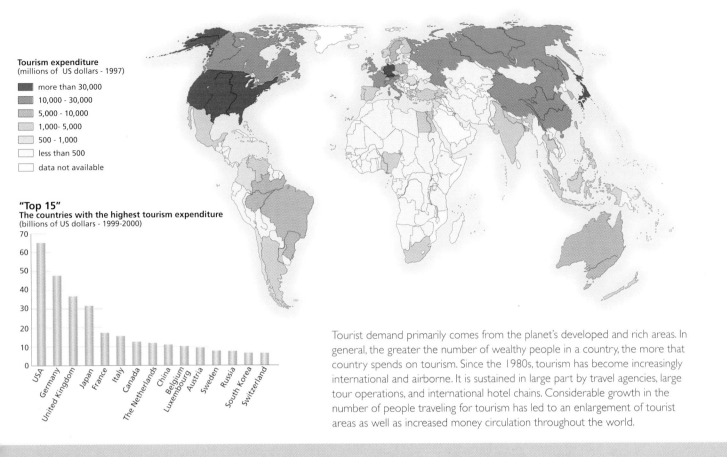

Tourism expenditure
(millions of US dollars - 1997)

- more than 30,000
- 10,000 - 30,000
- 5,000 - 10,000
- 1,000 - 5,000
- 500 - 1,000
- less than 500
- data not available

"Top 15"
The countries with the highest tourism expenditure
(billions of US dollars - 1999-2000)

Bar chart (vertical axis 0–70): USA, Germany, United Kingdom, Japan, France, Italy, Canada, The Netherlands, China, Belgium, Luxembourg, Austria, Sweden, Russia, South Korea, Switzerland

Tourist demand primarily comes from the planet's developed and rich areas. In general, the greater the number of wealthy people in a country, the more that country spends on tourism. Since the 1980s, tourism has become increasingly international and airborne. It is sustained in large part by travel agencies, large tour operations, and international hotel chains. Considerable growth in the number of people traveling for tourism has led to an enlargement of tourist areas as well as increased money circulation throughout the world.

focus**ON**

Religion and Tourism

Religious tourism is heavily present in many countries, especially in Catholic and Islamic ones. Journeys to holy places have ancient origins and date back to pilgrimages to ancient sanctuaries and Greek temples such as the famous one at Delphi. Today, religious tourism is a huge business, involving specialized travel agencies. In some countries, it is currently the most important form of tourism. For many people in India (who often have neither the financial means nor an interest in practicing Western-style tourism) a pilgrimage to the ancient sacred city of Varanasi (Benares) or to Mathura, the reputed birthplace of Lord Krishna, is an obligation, and people travel hundreds of miles across India to reach these sacred places of the Hindu religion. The same is true for Islamic believers and their traditional pilgrimage to Mecca, the birthplace of Mohammed.

Communication and Information
Fixed and Mobile Telephones

Many people claimed to have invented the first telephone, but Antonio Meucci may have created the first working phone in 1871, although it only worked over short distances. Patents for the first functional telephone were filed on February 14, 1876, by competing Americans Alexander Graham Bell and Elisha Gray. In 1878, the first telephone exchange opened in New Haven, Connecticut. In 1956, the first underwater cable between Europe and North America started to operate, allowing for 36 simultaneous telephone connections. Although invented just over a century ago, telephones have had continuous and innovative development, becoming a standard communication tool throughout the world and generating a variety of applications everywhere across the globe. Starting in the 1960s, satellite telecommunication systems further extended the possibilities of telephone communication. Satellites allow a greater volume of calls than land lines and cables, and provide full global connectivity. Increased use of cell phones has freed telephone communications from total dependence on a fixed network on the ground. These great technological innovations, together with deregulation of the markets—which, in almost all countries, has taken telephone service away from government or private monopolies—has led to a big drop in costs. This has promoted extension of global communications, with considerable benefits, especially for less developed countries.

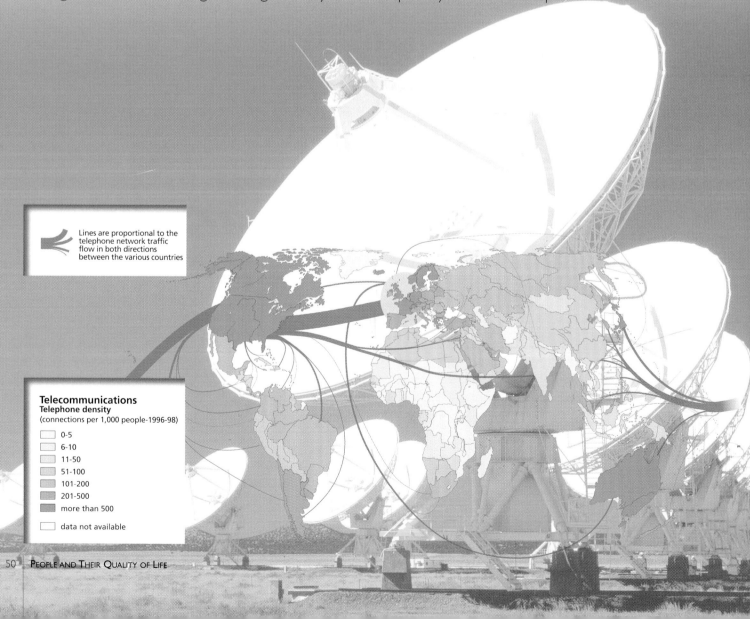

Lines are proportional to the telephone network traffic flow in both directions between the various countries

Telecommunications
Telephone density
(connections per 1,000 people-1996-98)

- 0-5
- 6-10
- 11-50
- 51-100
- 101-200
- 201-500
- more than 500

- data not available

Cellular Telephones - the Last Frontier

Cell phones are increasingly widespread because, thanks to their battery supply, small size, and light weight, users are free to connect with the telephone network even if they move around. In a cellular mobile network, coverage is obtained by dividing the service area into zones (cells) served by a radio transmitter to which the mobile phone connects. The new transmission systems are able to commute the radio channel automatically, enabling the user to move from one area to another without interrupting the communication.

In order to solve the problem of the different radio-mobile systems used in various countries and regions, the latest evolution in cell phones is the GSM system, which gives customers the ability to use the same phone in different networks and countries (*roaming*).

Cell phone companies continuously offer new services: calls to local data banks provide tourist or general information; access to address archives; the option to send alpha-numeric messages, pictures, and sounds; and

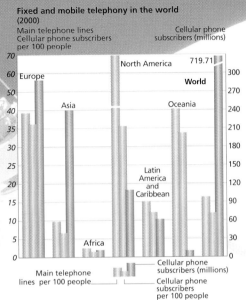

Fixed and mobile telephony in the world (2000)

Main telephone lines
Cellular phone subscribers per 100 people

Cellular phone subscribers (millions)

North America — 719.71
Europe
Asia
World
Oceania
Latin America and Caribbean
Africa

Main telephone lines per 100 people

Cellular phone subscribers (millions)
Cellular phone subscribers per 100 people

connection to computers and the Internet, which since the 1990s has revolutionized all aspects of global communication. Always available in a pocket or purse, cell phones now make it possible for people connect with one another, anywhere, anytime.

Perhaps the most freeing aspect of cell phone use is the fact that mobile

phones do not require the set-up and maintenance of expensive ground networks, which had often made telephones out of reach for many people in poorer countries, and also made phone service unreliable in countries with old networks. In much of Africa and in some Asian regions, wars have seriously damaged existing land telephone infrastructures. For these reasons, and because of their portability and convenience, in many countries the number of cell phones is much higher than the number of fixed phones.

Mobile communication
(cellular phones per 1,000 people - 1996/98)

- 0-1
- 2-10
- 11-50
- 51-100
- 101-200
- 201-400
- more than 400
- data not available

Communication Technology

People throughout the world now have a huge network of computers, a giant web of connections without space or time limits, which forms an information highway encircling the planet. This has created a new global communication channel: the Internet. It has revolutionized the way people conduct business, do research, and even do their shopping, which can now be done world-wide "on-line." Designed in the late 1960s by the U.S. Defense Department's Advanced Research Projects Agency (ARPA) in order to ensure that communications (and, therefore, military and government activities) could be maintained in the event of a nuclear attack, the Internet is based on packet communication technology. This means that information is grouped in "packets," which travel over fiber optics, copper, or radio links from one network node to another.

The first network had only four nodes and was called ARPANET. ARPANET was immediately successful and started to grow as more and more agencies and universities rapidly joined it. Indeed, researchers were the first to realize they had a magic instrument available, enabling them to exchange written information in real time.

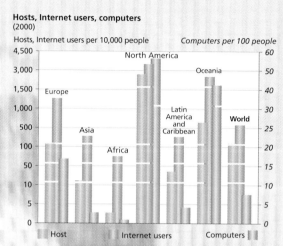

Hosts, Internet users, computers
(2000)

Hosts, Internet users per 10,000 people　　Computers per 100 people

Other networks developed in many different regions in the world, creating a complex web of connections. Startiing in 1990, the Internet has grown at an incredible pace. Estimates show that every year the Internet grows exponentially as the number of users increases along with the number of servers and the processing capacity of each server. Available in public libraries and cyber cafés as well as private sources, the Internet is increasingly available to all economic groups. Not owned by any entity, and free to all, the Internet is a globally available tool for communication and access to information.

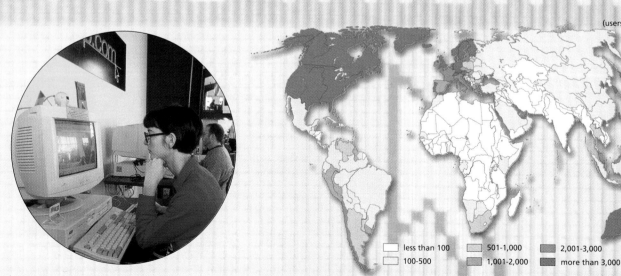

The Internet
(users per 10 000 people - 2001)

less than 100　　501-1,000　　2,001-3,000
100-500　　1,001-2,000　　more than 3,000

Dubai Internet City

In Dubai—a small state of the United Arab Emirates with 858,000 inhabitants and a far higher number of foreigners—an Internet city was officially opened on October 28, 2000. The city is entirely devoted to international commercial and industrial companies working online and in the electronic commerce sector.

Built in the desert in record time (completed in a year and a half), Dubai Internet City (DIC) offers its networks and services to the giant companies in this sector, which immediately opened their offices there. The large number of infrastructures (including gardens, artificial lakes, fountains, hotels, malls, sports and conference centers, and parking areas), and especially, the lack of any kind of taxation and extremely lean bureaucratic procedures, make Dubai Internet City a real competitor of the American Silicon Valley. It has the same potential, but much lower costs.

Dubai Internet City
- **Cost of the project completed so far:** 200 million U.S. dollars
- **Cost of the finished project:** 1 billion U.S. dollars
- **Surface:** 121,397 square feet (37,000 sq m)
- **Accepted companies:** 200
- **Applicant companies:** 350
- **Companies involved:** Microsoft, Canon, Hewlett-Packard, Oracle, Compaq, IBM, Dell, Siemens, Logica, Sony Ericsson, Cisco
- **Services:** broadband connections; local networks; research and development center; scientific and technological park; e-commerce, Internet University; design and management courses; easy recruitment of personnel (offer of specialized operators from all over the world, including India); service provider; instant technical support

India: Mine of Engineers

In India, 35% of the population lives on less than one dollar a day and 44.2% of the adults are illiterate. Nonetheless, this country is one of the world's major information technology districts and provides half the engineers required by U.S. software companies. Indian engineers speak English from an early age. Their salary is at least 25-50% lower than that of their American colleagues. It is thus not surprising that large international companies have decided to export their data processing activities to India. So, if you call an American software house for help, it is very likely that an Indian, and not an American, technician will answer the phone at the other end of the Internet.

Information Technology in India
- **University:** 7 prestigious technology and information technology institutes (IIT, Indian Institute of Technology) in Delhi, Kanpur, Kharagpur, Madras, Mumbai, Guwahati, and Roorkee
- **Higher Technical Institutes:** 3,000
- **Graduated engineers:** 240,000 a year
- **Certified IT technicians:** 1 million a year
- **Exported engineers:** 75,000 every year in the U.S.; 15,000 in Germany
- **Software companies:** 520
- **Value:** electronic consumables exports in 2000-2001 - 3.5 billion U.S. dollars -
- **Percentage:** electronic consumables exports over total exports in 2000-2001 - 7.9%
- **Government forecasts:** electronic consumables exports in 2008 – 50 billion U.S. dollars

What Kind of Wealth?
Official Wealth and Real Wealth

Globalization of the economy seems to offer considerable growth and development opportunities for all. In fact, there are still dramatic imbalances between wealthy and poor people, both at a world level (between one country and another) and within the countries themselves. The few rich people enjoy most of the national wealth and tend to get richer, while the poor, the overall majority, see their purchasing power continually decrease and their living conditions worsen.

In order to get a realistic view of a country's wealth, it is not enough to consider the per capita Gross Domestic Product (GDP). Wages and the country's cost of living need to be compared with that of other countries. In other words, it is necessary to assess salary purchasing power parity (PPP). In poor countries, rural areas are the most disadvantaged, because of such factors as rapid population growth, climatic variables that cause floods or droughts and famines, and the globalization of agriculture, which has in many cases destroyed traditional agricultural systems. Urban areas also have problems, as they must often absorb migrations and house society's least skilled people, who barely survive in shantytowns or slums.

North America
GDP
32.5 %

Latin America
and Caribbean
GDP
6.6 %

A fairly paid job, sufficient to support a family according to the well-being criteria in each community, enables individuals to feel they are an active part of the system in which they live and to have access to the numerous services that society can offer.

The Gross Domestic Product is an aggregate figure summarizing the economic results achieved by the various production sectors (primary, secondary, and tertiary) of a country. In the Southern Hemisphere, agriculture is the largest sector of the economy. In most Northern Hemisphere countries, the economy is driven by industry and services.

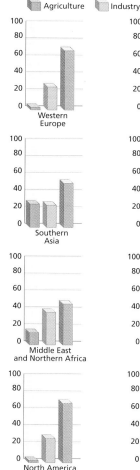

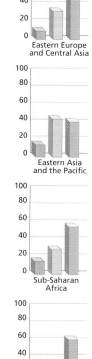

Distribution of Gross Domestic Product (GDP) by economic sectors (in % - 1999)

■ Agriculture ■ Industry ■ Services

Western Europe

Eastern Europe and Central Asia

Southern Asia

Eastern Asia and the Pacific

Middle East and Northern Africa

Sub-Saharan Africa

North America

Latin America and Caribbean

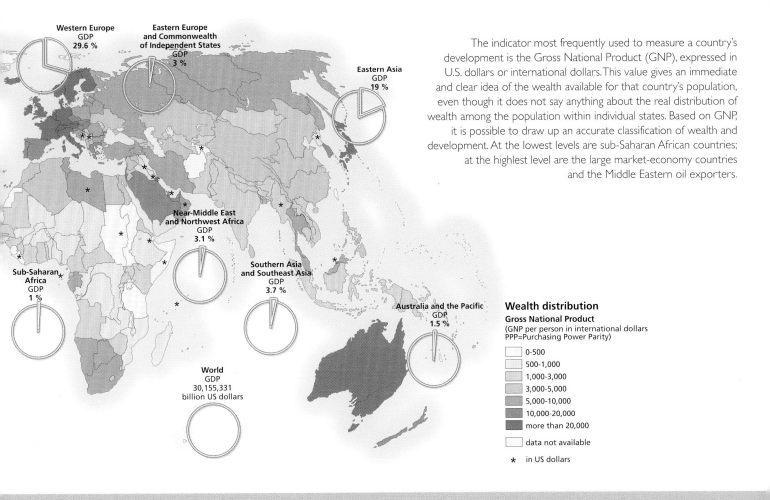

Western Europe
GDP
29.6 %

Eastern Europe
and Commonwealth
of Independent States
GDP
3 %

Eastern Asia
GDP
19 %

Near-Middle East
and Northwest Africa
GDP
3.1 %

Southern Asia
and Southeast Asia
GDP
3.7 %

Sub-Saharan
Africa
GDP
1 %

Australia and the Pacific
GDP
1.5 %

World
GDP
30,155,331
billion US dollars

The indicator most frequently used to measure a country's development is the Gross National Product (GNP), expressed in U.S. dollars or international dollars. This value gives an immediate and clear idea of the wealth available for that country's population, even though it does not say anything about the real distribution of wealth among the population within individual states. Based on GNP, it is possible to draw up an accurate classification of wealth and development. At the lowest levels are sub-Saharan African countries; at the highest level are the large market-economy countries and the Middle Eastern oil exporters.

Wealth distribution
Gross National Product
(GNP per person in international dollars
PPP=Purchasing Power Parity)

- 0-500
- 500-1,000
- 1,000-3,000
- 3,000-5,000
- 5,000-10,000
- 10,000-20,000
- more than 20,000

- data not available

* in US dollars

Hidden Inequality

The increasing inequality between nations has been accompanied, particularly in the last 15 or 20 years, by inequalities and imbalances inside the nations themselves. The difference between the income of the poorest 20% of the world's population and the income of the richest 20% of the population has moved up from 30:1 to 78:1 between 1960 and 1994.

The statistics dividing wealth by the number of people do not highlight the real distribution of income. The level of inequality in a specific economic system compared to a theoretical and even distribution is measured in thousandths by the Gini index, conceived by the Italian economist and statistician Corrado Gini. This indicator shows considerable variations at a global level and even between developed countries: zero indicates perfect equality, that is, a country where everybody has the same income, while one indicates absolute

inequality, that is, a country where the entire income is concentrated in the hands of one person. In poorer countries in particular, the gap between the majority of the population and the very few rich people is becoming increasingly wide. On one side there are excluded masses, who live on less than

one dollar a day and survive on subsistence agriculture. On the other side, a very small billionaire elite exploits the most profitable activities (plantations, exports, oil) and eats up national wealth, consumer goods, electricity, food, and drinking water.

**Wealth enjoyed by
the richest 20% of the population**
(% share of income or consumption)

- more than 60
- 50.1-60
- 40.1-50
- 30-40
- data not available

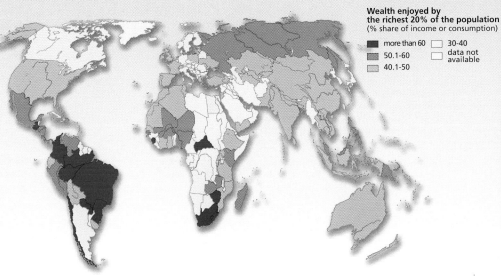

Wealth Measures
Family Assets and Consumption

The first major change in the ways people acquired consumer items took place at the end of the 19th century, when the distribution of goods moved from the craftsman's workshop to shops and then to department stores. Another milestone coincided with the post-World War II economic boom of the 1950s and 1960s that deeply transformed social life, first in the United States and then in all industrialized countries, challenging social values and lifestyles. The world has come out of a mainly agricultural economy and society, characterized by a single family-income and the ethic of saving, and has entered the industrial and consumer economy and society, dominated by the urban, multi-income family, and buying on credit.

The fast spread of technological innovations and distribution networks has made a large quantity of goods available, from refrigerators, televisions, dishwashers, and cars, to computers, CD players, faxes and other electronic appliances.

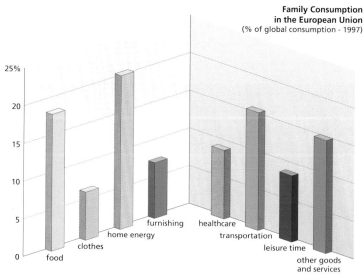

**Family Consumption
in the European Union**
(% of global consumption - 1997)

One way of measuring people's assets is by comparing the amount and quality of their consumer goods. While this comparison does not measure any person's true quality of life (which includes leisure time, health, and personal connections, among other factors) consumer goods are one indicator of a people's relative abundance or poverty.

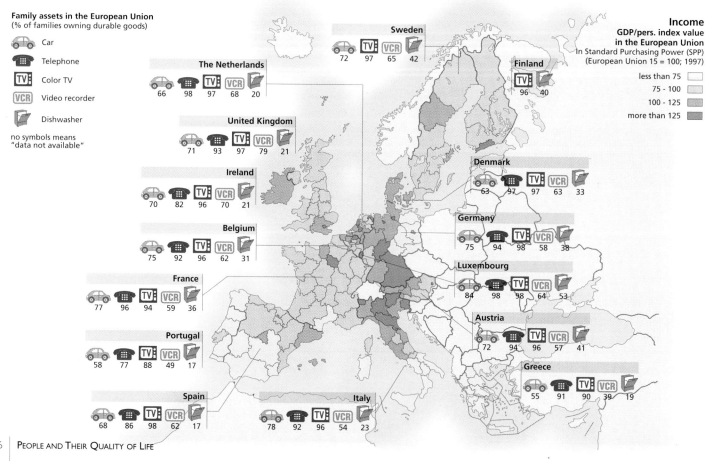

Family assets in the European Union
(% of families owning durable goods)

- Car
- Telephone
- Color TV
- Video recorder
- Dishwasher

no symbols means
"data not available"

Income
GDP/pers. index value
in the European Union
In Standard Purchasing Power (SPP)
(European Union 15 = 100; 1997)

- less than 75
- 75 - 100
- 100 - 125
- more than 125

Sweden 72 97 65 42
The Netherlands 66 98 97 68 20
Finland 96 40
United Kingdom 71 93 97 79 21
Ireland 70 82 96 70 21
Denmark 63 97 97 63 33
Belgium 75 92 96 62 31
Germany 75 94 98 58 38
Luxembourg 84 98 98 64 53
France 77 96 94 59 36
Austria 72 94 96 57 41
Portugal 58 77 88 49 17
Greece 55 91 90 39 19
Spain 68 86 98 62 17
Italy 78 92 96 54 23

focusN

One World, Many Worlds

Expansion of the middle class and the consumer society has been accompanied by the development of globalized information. This combination tends to bring a single economic, cultural, and lifestyle model to the entire world. This has led consumerism to cross national borders and has resulted in "Americanization"—first of Western Europe, then of other countries—and to the internationalization of fashions. Obviously, the possibility of owning goods directly depends on personal and family incomes and is not enjoyed by the poorer countries where the main concerns are surviving or freeing oneself from misery. In spite of this trend to global consumerism and "Americanization" of the world, many differences remain. The extremely different types of goods identified by statistical surveys in various countries show different levels of development and lifestyles that reflect local situations, traditions, activities, the climate, and general conditions of a country.

USA
Ownership of durable goods
(% of families - 1997)

Type of household electronic appliances	% of families
Washing machine	77.4
Tumble dryer	71.1
Dishwasher	50.2
Air conditioner	73.2
Fan	60.1
Refrigerator	99.9
Freezer	33.2
Stove	99.2
Microwave oven	83
Water heater	100
Color TV	98.7
Video recorder	87.6
Stereo system	68.8
Cordless phone	61.4
Answering machine	58.4
PC	35
Fax	6.2
Photocopying machine	3.7

Brazil
Ownership of durable goods
(% of families - 1997)

Type of household electronic appliance	% of the total number of families	% of families living in cities	% of families living in the countryside
Washing machine	30.4	35.3	9.3
Refrigerator	78.2	86.4	43.2
Freezer	18	19.3	12.3
Stove	96.6	98.3	89.2
Water filter	58.1	61.5	43.3
Radio	90.4	91.9	83.9
Color TV	69.2	77.9	32
Black-and-white TV	15.1	13.4	22.2

The average American family has an enormous quantity of goods. U.S. statistics do not even take into account black-and-white TVs or traditional telephones, but, rather, color TVs and cordless phones. In Brazil, there are still many black-and-white TVs, and a water filter is still considered an important item in the average household.

Droughts, famines, and conflicts are devastating many African countries. In many communities, families first must solve survival issues, then scrape some money together to buy seeds and a few cattle, and then pay school fees for their children. Many people in African countries make their own baskets and sew their own clothes. Radios and the batteries required for them are often considered a luxury.

China is a country characterized by marked differences between its urban and rural lifestyles. People living in large cities tend to add many aspects of Western lifestyle to daily life, while those living in the countryside have limited resources and less exposure to Western influence, and therefore tend to follow more traditional styles of dress and lifestyle. Across the country, an object like a sewing machine, often taken for granted in the West, is highly valued as a family asset.

China
Ownership of durable goods
(every 100 families)

Type of household electronic appliance	Type of consumer good		Type of household electronic appliance	Type of consumer good	
	Urban fam.	Rural fam.		Urban fam.	Rural fam.
Washing machine	78	-	Color TV	59	5
Refrigerator	42	-	Black-and-white TV	52	40
Electrical fan	135	-	Recorder	80	-
Sewing machine	70	55	Bicycle	189	118
Radio	45	45	Wrist watch	299	172

Poverty and Misery

Over one billion people survive on a dollar a day;
2.8 billion live on less than two dollars; two billion
people have no access to safe drinking water; and
a minimum of three million children die every year
because of malnutrition. In developing countries
the poor represent one-third of the population.
The African regions south of the Sahara are the
poorest and most desperate areas in the world.

For people living in these countries, even surviving
becomes a fierce struggle. Infant mortality rates are
extremely high. Life expectancy is shorter. Thirst and
hunger; inadequate housing; and lack of services,
health care, and schools are the most obvious
features of general, dire poverty.

Misery creates a vicious circle, because it
undermines people's ability to work and produce
(when it does not cause their death) and, therefore,
impairs their ability to improve their own income
and contribute to the wealth of their country.
Moreover, poor people are particularly vulnerable
to natural disasters and conflicts, which are more
disruptive in economically weak countries than they
are in countries that can afford to take precautions.

Children, more than any other category of people, suffer the
consequences of economic underdevelopment the most. The figures
published by UNICEF are alarming—one child out of four today lives
in conditions of extreme misery. In developing countries, the ratio goes
up to one child out of three. Every three seconds a child dies because
of poverty. One out of twelve dies before reaching the age of five.

The poorest countries in the world
International poverty threshold
(% of population living
on one US dollar a day)

0 10 20 30 40 50 60 70 80 90 100

Ghana
Mali
Zambia
Nigeria
Central African Rep.
Niger
Burkina Faso
Sierra Leone
Gambia
India
Lesotho
Honduras
Guatemala
Mozambique
Nepal
Uganda
Zimbabwe
Rwanda
Namibia
Botswana
Ethiopia

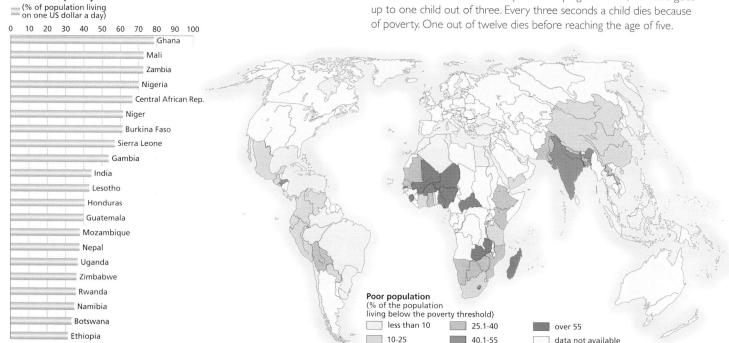

Poor population
(% of the population
living below the poverty threshold)

less than 10	25.1-40	over 55
10-25	40.1-55	data not available

Poverty in Rich Countries

A person is defined as poor if his/her income is below a level considered the minimum required to meet vital needs. This level is called the "poverty threshold." In industrialized countries, over 100 million people—47 million of whom are children—live below this threshold.

There are more than 37 million unemployed. The reductions in social expenditure made by many countries have worsened the quality of life for economically weaker classes. As a consequence, even those who are not at the lowest levels have to face very difficult situations and social exclusion. Losing one's job or having a low salary often means not being able to buy consumer goods, books, papers, or magazines; limits access to new technologies and cultural events; and restricts educational opportunities. Job loss can also hinder social relations and sometimes means losing respectability. Poor families in rich countries cannot go on vacation or send their children to

camp the way others in their country can. They are less able to help their children after school, nor can they afford to enroll them in higher education. In some countries, poor families do not even have access to health care services. These conditions lead to exclusion of the poor from the social system and lifestyle of the middle and upper classes of their society.

In the suburbs or large cities there are pockets of hopeless misery and exclusion: an "underdevelopment within development" phenomenon that especially hits the unemployed, immigrants, the elderly, and children. There are 18 million street children in India, 40 million in Latin America, and over 100 million all over the world. Their problems affect the quality of life for all citizens of a society.

Poverty in rich countries
(% of the population below the national poverty threshold earning less than 11 or 4 US dollars/day)

Country	- 11 US $ /day	Country	- 11 US $ /day - 4 US $ /day*
Norway	4	France	10
Australia	18	United Kingdom	16
Canada	7	Germany	7
Sweden	6	Hungary	4*
USA	14	Poland	20*
The Netherlands	7	Estonia	37*
Finland	5	Lithuania	30*

According to the most recent UN Food and Agriculture Organization (FAO) summit, 800 million people in the world are starving. In particular, about half the children in developing countries, especially in sub-Saharan Africa, are undernourished, or their diet lacks proteins (mainly proteins of animal origin) and elements which are necessary for their growth.

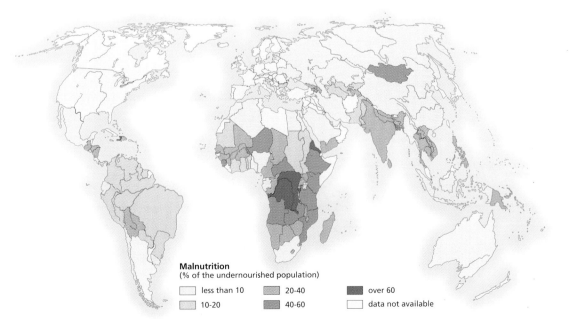

Malnutrition
(% of the undernourished population)

- less than 10
- 10-20
- 20-40
- 40-60
- over 60
- data not available

Hunger and underdevelopment
(% of children aged between 0 and 5)

underweight — rickets sufferers

60 50 40 30 20 10 0

Bangladesh
India
Cambodia
Niger
Nepal
Ethiopia
Yemen
Eritrea
Maldives
Angola
Madagascar
Laos
Mali
Chad
Vietnam
Myanmar
Bhutan
Burundi
Burkina Faso
Congo, Dem. Rep.
Indonesia

The Poor's Debt
An Increasingly Heavy Burden

Extensive borrowing abroad, practiced by most developing countries, originated during the oil crisis of 1973-74. The large increase in oil prices at that time ensured exporting countries enormous revenues (so-called oil-dollars), which they placed on the international market through large banks. These banks offered the money to developing countries, which mainly invested it to build infrastructures aimed at supporting their exports of agricultural and mining raw materials, whose prices, however, dropped significantly in the following years. Some developing countries simply borrowed money to purchase oil, and failed to invest in their infrastructures at all.

Then, in 1979, the oil price rocketed again, reaching 20 times that of 1973. In order to tackle inflation, the U.S. and British governments increased interest rates. The countries which had borrowed money at a 5% interest rate now had to pay rates up to over 30%. Moreover, the U. S. dollar value doubled between 1979 and 1980 against the Deutsch Mark and the British Pound and shot up against currencies of underdeveloped

countries. The interest for one year, expressed in national currencies, became higher than the total borrowed capital. Mexico was the first, in 1982, to announce its inability to pay its debt. Banks, therefore, decided to turn the expired debt installments into further loans, but at higher interest rates. A borrowing spiral was thus triggered, which continues today and remains a real barrier to development.

The burden of debt
Borrowing abroad (% of the GDP - 1998)

- 0-15
- 15-30
- 30-45
- 45-60
- 60-75
- 75-100
- 100-125
- 125-150
- 150-200
- more than 200

- data not available

The countries most heavily in debt
(billions of US dollars - 1999)

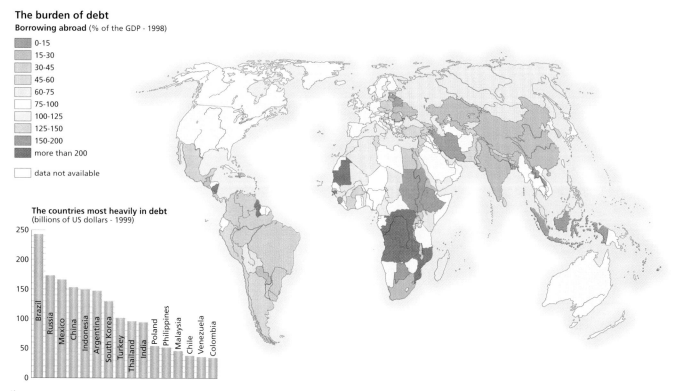

World Welfare: Aid for Development

International aid decisively contributes to sustaining the development of poor countries. That aid is most valuable when it is aimed at building infrastructures and creating basic knowledge and skills at a local level, so that the local population can promote its own growth. Unfortunately, in 2001 the overall amount of aid for development was 20% lower than in 1990, when, after the end of the cold war, the *Official Development Assistance* (ODA) suffered the heaviest cuts.

Donor countries' foreign politics often play a significant role in the amount of aid given. By some estimates, Israel ranks third in the world, after Cap Verde and Belize, in terms of the amount of per capita aid received. Although it is one of the wealthiest countries in the world, Egypt's seven billion dollar debt with the United States was canceled in exchange for its support to the Gulf War in 1991. This situation highlights the importance of the appeal launched by the European Union—which finances more than half the current international aid at a global

level—to agree upon a common strategy among industrialized countries in order to achieve two main objectives: reducing poverty and gradually integrating developing countries into the world economy.

The aid flow

Main donor countries	Aid for development (1999)		To the poorest countries (*)
	% of GDP	million US $	
Denmark	1.01	1,733	32
Norway	0.91	1,370	33
The Netherlands	0.79	3,134	20
Sweden	0.7	1,630	25
Luxembourg	0.66	119	25
France	0.39	5,637	16
Japan	0.35	15,323	17
Switzerland	0.35	969	27
Finland	0.33	416	25
Ireland	0.31	245	37
Belgium	0.3	760	22
Canada	0.28	1,699	18
New Zealand	0.27	134	24
Germany	0.26	1,370	20
Australia	0.26	982	17
Austria	0.26	527	14
Portugal	0.26	276	45
United Kingdom	0.23	3,401	21
Spain	0.23	1,363	11
Italy	0.15	1,806	22
Greece	0.15	194	2
USA	0.1	9,145	16

(*) % of total aid granted

The aid granted by industrialized countries or international institutions (such as the European Central Bank, whose headquarters is picturerd above) to underdeveloped countries consists of loans, donations, technical and scientific support, and international commercial benefits. Humanitarian aid, instead, is targeted at the populations hit by natural disasters or conflicts and consists of goods and services (such as food, drugs, and earth-removing operations).

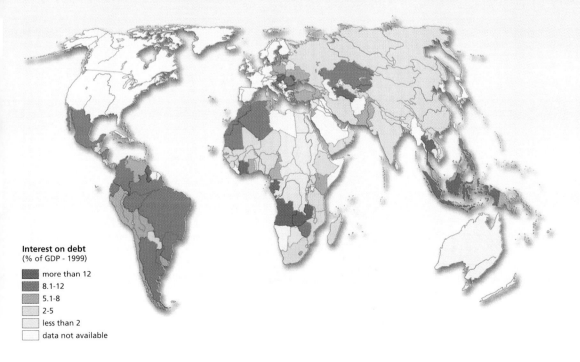

Interest on debt
(% of GDP - 1999)

- more than 12
- 8.1-12
- 5.1-8
- 2-5
- less than 2
- data not available

The United Nations estimates that if the resources used to pay back debt were employed for health and education, seven million children could be saved every year. This comes to 134,000 children every week. In the last few years the leading countries seem to have started to realize that canceling or reducing debts to a sustainable level will enable poor countries to allocate resources to finance their development and improve the life of their people.

Aid and the Human Family

Aid granted
(1997-98)
Donor countries
(amount in US $ per person)

- less than 30
- 30-50
- 50-100
- 100-200
- 200-300
- more than 300

Aid received
(1997-98)
Receiving countries
(amount in US $ per person)

- less than 5
- 5-10
- 10-30
- 30-50
- 50-100
- 100-200
- more than 200
- data not available

Refugees

→ Refugee migrations

Main hosting countries (each square corresponds to 50,000 refugees)

Canada

United Kingdom

The Netherland

France

Switzerland

Denmar

North America

United States

MINURSO

Latin America and Caribbean

UNAMS

Guinea

Côte d'Ivoire

Uganda

Africa

Cong Dem. R

World refugees depending on the UNHCR
United Nations High Commissioner for Refugees
(in millions of people)

1990	
1991	
1992	
1993	
1994	
1995	
1996	
1997	
1998	
1999	
2000	
2001	

(scale: 0, 5, 10, 15, 20, 25, 30)

Development funds
(% of total aid offered)

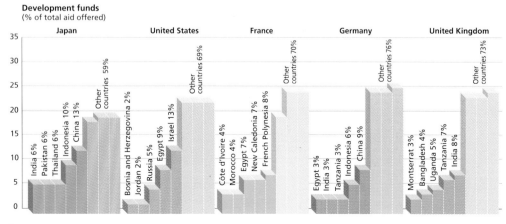

Japan: India 6%, Pakistan 6%, Thailand 6%, Indonesia 10%, China 13%, Other countries 59%

United States: Bosnia and Herzegovina 2%, Jordan 2%, Russia 5%, Egypt 9%, Israel 13%, Other countries 69%

France: Côte d'Ivoire 4%, Morocco 4%, Egypt 7%, New Caledonia 7%, French Polynesia 8%, Other countries 70%

Germany: Egypt 3%, India 3%, Tanzania 3%, Indonesia 6%, China 9%, Other countries 76%

United Kingdom: Montserrat 3%, Bangladesh 4%, Uganda 5%, Tanzania 7%, India 8%, Other countries 73%

(scale: 0, 5, 10, 15, 20, 25, 30, 35)

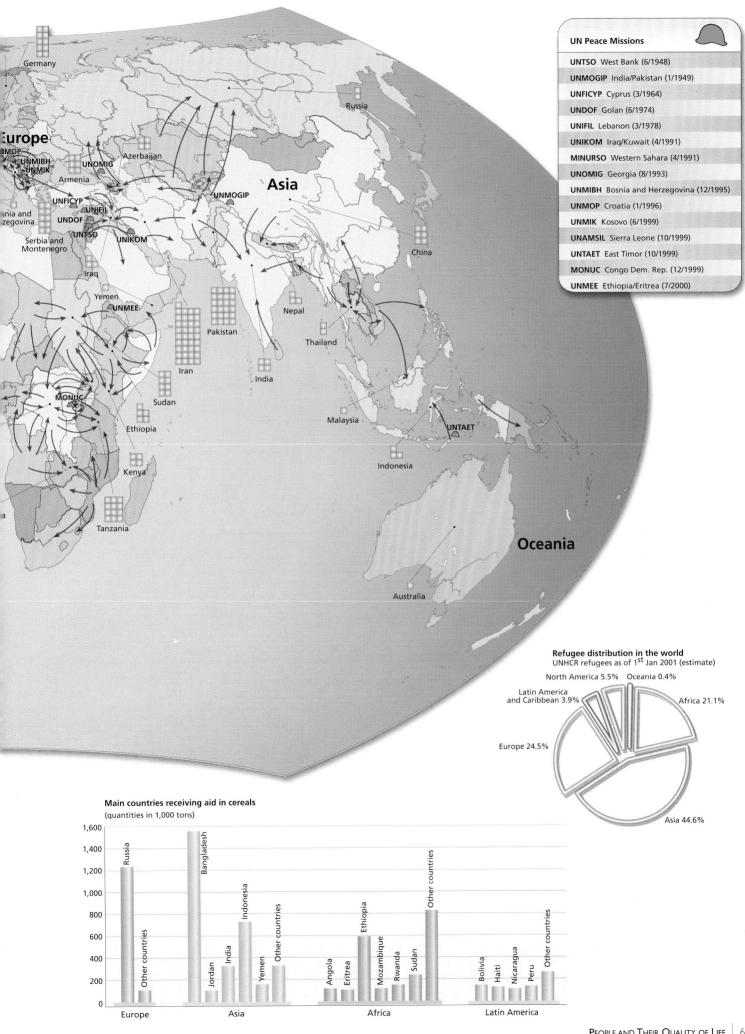

Germany

Russia

Europe

UNMOP
UNMIBH
UNMIK
UNOMIG
Armenia
Azerbaijan
UNFICYP
UNIFIL
Bosnia and
Herzegovina
UNDOF
UNTSO
Serbia and
Montenegro
UNIKOM
Iraq
Yemen
UNMEE
MONUC
Ethiopia
Kenya
Tanzania

Asia

UNMOGIP

China

Nepal

Pakistan

Thailand

Iran

India

Sudan

Malaysia

UNTAET

Indonesia

Oceania

Australia

UN Peace Missions

UNTSO	West Bank (6/1948)
UNMOGIP	India/Pakistan (1/1949)
UNFICYP	Cyprus (3/1964)
UNDOF	Golan (6/1974)
UNIFIL	Lebanon (3/1978)
UNIKOM	Iraq/Kuwait (4/1991)
MINURSO	Western Sahara (4/1991)
UNOMIG	Georgia (8/1993)
UNMIBH	Bosnia and Herzegovina (12/1995)
UNMOP	Croatia (1/1996)
UNMIK	Kosovo (6/1999)
UNAMSIL	Sierra Leone (10/1999)
UNTAET	East Timor (10/1999)
MONUC	Congo Dem. Rep. (12/1999)
UNMEE	Ethiopia/Eritrea (7/2000)

Refugee distribution in the world
UNHCR refugees as of 1st Jan 2001 (estimate)

North America 5.5%   Oceania 0.4%

Latin America
and Caribbean 3.9%

Africa 21.1%

Europe 24.5%

Asia 44.6%

Main countries receiving aid in cereals
(quantities in 1,000 tons)

Europe: Russia, Other countries
Asia: Bangladesh, Jordan, India, Indonesia, Yemen, Other countries
Africa: Angola, Eritrea, Ethiopia, Mozambique, Rwanda, Sudan, Other countries
Latin America: Bolivia, Haiti, Nicaragua, Peru, Other countries

COUNTRIES	HDI ranking/value (1)	Life expectancy M/F (2)	GNP/pers. (US $) (3)	Enrollments at primary school % M/F (4)	Work force by sector % (5)
Afghanistan	-	45/46	-	42/15	67/6/27
Albania	85/0.7	70/76	3,189	100/100	50/29/21
Algeria	100/0.7	68/70	5,063	94/91	25/30/45
Andorra	-	-	-	-	1/21/78
Angola	146/0.4	45/48	3,179	-	68/11/21
Antigua and Barbuda	-	-	-	-	4/17/29
Argentina	34/0.8	70/77	12,227	96/96	12/31/57
Armenia	72/0.7	67/74	2,215	-	41/22/37
Australia	2/0.9	75/81	24,574	95/95	5/22/73
Austria	16/0.9	74/80	25,089	90/91	6/31/63
Azerbaijan	79/0.7	66/74	2,850	89/90	23/11/66
Bahamas	42/0.8	-	15,258	99/99	-
Bahrain	40/0.8	-	13,688	96/98	2/25/73
Bangladesh	132/0.5	58/58	1,483	80/83	59/10/31
Barbados	31/0.9	-	14,353	100/100	4/21/75
Belarus	53/0.8	62/74	6,876	87/84	16/35/49
Belgium	5/0.9	74/81	25,443	99/98	2/27/71
Belize	54/0.8	73/76	4,959	90/86	-
Benin	147/0.4	52/55	933	75/50	57/11/32
Bhutan	130/0.5	60/62	1,341	58/47	94/1/5
Bolivia	104/0.6	60/63	2,355	95/87	43/18/39
Bosnia and Herzegovina	-	71/76	-	100/100	14/21/65
Botswana	114/0.6	46/48	6,872	98/99	16/26/58
Brazil	69/0.7	63/71	7,037	-	23/20/57
Brunei	32/0.9	-	17,868	90/91	2/21/77
Bulgaria	57/0.8	68/75	5,071	98/98	27/29/44
Burkina Faso	159/0.3	44/45	965	40/28	92/2/6
Burundi	160/0.3	41/44	160	38/37	93/2/5
Cambodia	121/0.5	51/55	1,361	82/74	71/7/22
Cameroon	125/0.5	53/56	1,573	82/71	63/7/30
Canada	3/0.9	76/82	26,251	96/94	3/23/74
Cape Verde	91/0.7	-	4,490	100/97	25/25/50
Central African Republic	154/0.4	43/47	1,166	51/27	80/4/16

COUNTRIES	HDI ranking/value (1)	Life expectancy M/F (2)	GNP/pers. (US $) (3)	Enrollments at primary school % M/F (4)	Work force by sector % (5)
Chad	155/0.4	46/49	850	65/39	83/2/15
Chile	39/0.8	72/78	8,652	88/88	14/26/60
China	87/0.7	68/72	3,617	99/99	50/24/26
Colombia	62/0.8	67/74	5,749	-	22/20/58
Comoros	124/0.5	-	1,429	65/55	77/9/14
Congo	126/0.5	46/51	727	99/99	44/13/43
Congo, Democratic Rep.	142/0.4	49/56	801	66/51	65/16/19
Costa Rica	41/0.8	74/79	8,860	93/93	20/23/57
Croatia	46/0.8	69/77	7,387	93/96	17/30/53
Cuba	-	74/78	-	94/95	18/30/52
Cyprus	25/0.9	-	19,006	96/96	10/23/67
Czech Republic	33/0.8	70/77	13,018	87/87	5/41/54
Denmark	15/0.3	73/78	25,869	99/99	4/26/70
Djibouti	137/0.4	-	2,377	39/28	75/11/14
Dominica	-	-	-	89/89	31/20/49
Dominican Republic	86/0.8	69/73	5,507	84/85	20/25/55
East Timor	-	-	304	-	-
Ecuador	84/0.7	67/72	2,994	90/91	31/18/51
Egypt	105/0.6	65/68	3,420	94/89	29/23/48
El Salvador	95/0.7	67/73	4,344	94/89	26/24/50
Equatorial Guinea	110/0.6	48/52	4,676	89/89	75/5/20
Eritrea	148/0.4	49/52	880	40/35	-
Estonia	44/0.8	63/75	8,355	87/86	12/32/56
Ethiopia	158/0.3	42/44	628	43/28	86/2/12
Fiji	67/0.8	71/75	4,799	99/100	37/35/28
Finland	10/0.9	73/81	23,096	98/98	6/28/66
France	13/0.9	74/82	22,897	100/100	4/25/71
Gabon	109/0.6	-	6,024	82/83	42/12/46
Gambia	149/0.4	45/49	1,580	64/55	73/10/17
Georgia	76/0.7	69/77	2,431	95/95	30/20/50
Germany	17/0.9	74/80	23,742	86/87	3/34/63
Ghana	119/0.5	58/62	1,881	-	59/13/28
Greece	23/0.9	76/81	15,414	90/90	18/23/59

COUNTRIES	HDI ranking/value (1)	Life expectancy M/F (2)	GNP/pers. (US $) (3)	Enrollments at primary school % M/F (4)	Work force by sector % (5)
Grenada	-	-	-	98/97	17/22/61
Guatemala	108/0.6	61/67	3,674	81/75	58/18/24
Guinea	150/0.4	46/47	1,934	49/30	71/2/27
Guinea-Bissau	156/0.3	43/46	678	58/32	77/5/18
Guyana	93/0.7	61/68	3,640	89/84	22/25/53
Haiti	134/0.5	51/56	1,464	66/66	57/9/34
Honduras	107/0.6	68/72	2,340	85/86	37/22/41
Hungary	36/0.8	67/75	11,430	97/96	7/34/59
Iceland	7/0.9	77/81	27,835	98/98	9/24/67
India	115/0.6	62/63	2,248	78/64	61/19/20
Indonesia	102/0.7	63/67	2,857	97/93	41/19/40
Iran	90/0.7	69/70	5,531	99/94	23/31/46
Iraq	-	61/64	-	98/88	16/18/66
Ireland	18/0.9	74/79	25,918	100/100	8/29/63
Israel	22/0.9	76/80	18,440	-	2/27/71
Italy	20/0.9	75/81	22,172	100/100	5/32/63
Ivory Coast (Côted'Ivoire)	144/0.4	46/47	1,654	63/47	51/12/37
Jamaica	78/0.7	73/77	3,561	89/87	22/19/59
Japan	9/1	77/83	24,898	100/100	5/32/63
Jordan	88/0.7	69/72	3,955	86/86	6/18/76
Kazakhstan	75/0.7	63/72	4,915	100/100	22/15/63
Kenya	123/0.5	51/53	1,022	92/89	75/10/15
Kiribati	-	-	-	-	71/3/26
Korea, North	-	69/75	-	-	38/31/31
Korea, South	27/0.9	69/76	15,712	97/98	11/28/61
Kuwait	43/0.8	74/78	17,289	89/85	2/23/75
Kyrgyzstan	92/0.7	63/72	2,573	98/97	48/17/35
Laos	131/0.5	52/55	1,471	80/72	77/7/16
Latvia	50/0.8	62/74	6,264	88/92	18/24/58
Lebanon	65/0.8	68/72	4,705	-	14/27/59
Lesotho	120/0.5	55/57	1,854	55/65	39/29/32
Liberia	-	46/49	-	43/31	68/8/24
Libya	59/0.8	68/72	7,570	97/96	18/30/52

COUNTRIES	HDI ranking/value (1)	Life expectancy M/F (2)	GNP/pers. (US $) (3)	Enrollments at primary school % M/F (4)	Work force by sector % (5)
Liechtenstein	-	-	-	-	2/37/61
Lithuania	47/0.8	64/76	6,656	-	21/28/51
Luxembourg	12/0.9	-	42,769	84/86	2/25/73
Macedonia	60/0.8	71/75	4,651	97/96	19/34/47
Madagascar	135/0.5	56/59	799	67/69	82/5/13
Malawi	151/0.4	39/40	586	100/100	87/5/8
Malaysia	56/0.8	70/74	8,209	95/96	17/37/46
Maldives	77/0.7	-	4,423	93/92	-
Mali	153/0.4	52/55	753	47/33	83/6/11
Malta	30/0.9	-	15,189	100/100	2/26/72
Marshall Islands	-	-	-	100/100	-
Mauritania	139/0.4	52/55	1,609	61/35	62/12/26
Mauritius	63/0.8	-	9,107	97/99	12/38/50
Mexico	51/0.8	70/75	8,297	100/100	23/24/53
Micronesia	-	-	-	-	-
Moldova	98/0.7	64/72	2,037	-	40/17/43
Monaco	-	-	-	-	-
Mongolia	116/0.6	64/67	1,711	93/94	49/12/39
Morocco	112/0.6	65/69	3,419	77/64	40/23/37
Mozambique	157/0.3	44/47	861	47/40	81/6/13
Myanmar	118/0.6	59/62	1,027	-	66/12/22
Namibia	111/0.6	52/53	5,468	84/88	48/15/37
Nauru	-	-	-	99/97	-
Nepal	129/0.5	58/57	1,237	79/60	81/3/16
Netherlands	8/0.9	75/81	24,215	100/99	3/22/75
New Zealand	19/0.9	74/80	19,104	100/100	9/23/68
Nicaragua	106/0.6	66/71	2,279	76/79	42/17/41
Niger	161/0.3	47/50	753	30/19	89/4/7
Nigeria	136/0.5	49/52	853	38/33	43/7/50
Norway	1/0.9	75/81	28,433	100/100	5/22/73
Oman	71/0.7	69/73	13,356	86/86	9/28/63
Pakistan	127/0.5	63/65	1,834	84/60	44/19/37
Palau	-	-	-	-	9/14/77

COUNTRIES	HDI ranking/value (1)	Life expectancy M/F (2)	GNP/pers. (US $) (3)	Enrollments at primary school % M/F (4)	Work force by sector % (5)
Panama	52/0.8	72/76	5,875	91/91	18/18/64
Papua New Guinea	122/0.5	57/59	2,367	79/67	79/7/14
Paraguay	80/0.7	67/72	4,384	91/92	32/19/49
Peru	73/0.7	66/71	4,622	100/100	33/17/50
Philippines	70/0.7	67/70	3,805	98/93	39/15/46
Poland	38/0.8	68/77	8,450	95/94	19/32/49
Portugal	28/0.9	72/79	16,064	100/100	13/36/51
Qatar	48/0.8	-	18,789	96/92	-
Romania	58/0.8	66/74	6,041	92/91	37/32/31
Russia	55/0.8	61/73	7,473	93/93	13/31/56
Rwanda	152/0.4	39/42	885	67/68	90/3/7
Samoa	96/0.7	-	4,047	94/91	-
San Marino	-	-	-	-	1/41/58
São Tomé and Príncipe	-	-	-	-	40/16/44
Saudi Arabia	68/0.8	70/73	10,815	81/73	13/23/64
Senegal	145/0.4	51/54	1,419	65/55	65/8/27
Serbia and Montenegro	-	70/75	-	69/70	3/30/67
Seychelles	-	-	-	100/100	6/22/72
Sierra Leone	162/0.3	36/39	448	-	62/18/20
Singapore	26/0.9	75/79	20,767	93/92	-/28/72
Slovakia	35/0.8	69/77	10,591	-	7/38/55
Slovenia	29/0.9	71/78	15,977	95/94	11/38/51
Solomon Islands	-	70/74	-	-	27/14/59
Somalia	-	45/49	-	13/7	71/10/19
South Africa	94/0.7	52/58	8,908	88/86	11/25/64
Spain	21/0.9	75/82	18,079	100/100	7/31/62
Sri Lanka	81/0.7	71/75	3,729	-	35/22/43
St. Kitts and Nevis	-	-	-	92/86	-
St. Lucia	-	-	-	-	-
St. Vincent and the Grenadines	-	-	-	90/78	-
Sudan	138/0.4	54/56	664	43/37	69/8/23
Suriname	64/0.8	68/73	4,178	100/100	20/24/56
Swaziland	113/0.6	-	3,987	100/100	39/22/39

COUNTRIES	HDI ranking/value (1)	Life expectancy M/F (2)	GNP/pers. (US $) (3)	Enrollments at primary school % M/F (4)	Work force by sector % (5)
Sweden	4/0.9	76/81	22,636	100/100	3/25/72
Switzerland	11/0.9	75/82	27,171	96/96	4/26/70
Syria	97/0.7	67/71	4,454	96/92	26/23/51
Taiwan	-	-	-	-	9/38/53
Tajikistan	103/0.7	64/70	1,031	-	65/11/24
Tanzania	140/0.4	47/49	501	56/57	80/5/15
Thailand	66/0.8	66/72	6,132	82/79	49/18/33
Togo	128/0.5	48/70	1,410	85/61	68/12/20
Tonga	-	-	-	98/93	-
Trinidad and Tobago	49/0.8	72/76	8,176	88/88	8/28/64
Tunisia	89/0.7	68/71	5,957	97/94	22/34/44
Turkey	82/0.7	67/72	6,380	93/82	39/25/36
Turkmenistan	83/0.7	62/69	3,347	-	48/18/34
Tuvalu	-	-	-	100/100	-
Uganda	141/0.4	39/40	1,167	92/83	80/6/14
Ukraine	74/0.7	64/74	3,458	-	26/26/48
United Arab Emirates	45/0.8	74/76	18,162	98/98	8/35/57
United Kingdom	14/0.9	75/80	22,093	97/98	2/23/75
United States	6/0.9	73/80	31,872	94/95	3/23/74
Uruguay	37/0.8	70/78	8,879	93/93	4/25/71
Uzbekistan	99/0.7	64/71	2,251	87/89	40/19/41
Vanuatu	-	-	-	76/72	-
Vatican City	-	-	-	-	-
Venezuela	61/0.8	70/76	5,495	83/85	10/24/66
Vietnam	101/0.7	65/70	1,860	95/94	67/13/20
Yemen	133/0.5	57/58	806	79/39	57/10/33
Zambia	143/0.4	40/41	756	85/86	71/7/22
Zimbabwe	117/0.6	44/45	2,876	87/87	66/10/24
WORLD	..	63/68	..	85/78	..

(1) **HDI** Human Development Index, expressed by a country's ranking in the world classification and the related values in thousandths. The values have been rounded in this chart.

(2) **Life Expectancy** Average number of years that a person can expect to live at birth (M/F males/females)

(3) **GNP/pers.** Gross National Product per person, expressed in U.S. dolllars ($)

- data not available

(4) **Enrollment at primary school** Percentage of children enrolled at primary school (M/F males/females) out of the total number of children in the age bracket corresponding to primary school

(5) **Work force by sector** Percentage of a country's working-age population, employed in the primary/secondary/tertiary sectors, respectively

.. data not quantifiable

Glossary

A

Acquired Immune Deficiency Syndrome (AIDS)
A viral disease, currently of epidemic proportions, which seriously weakens the immune system, exposing the patient to extremely high risk of contracting infections and other diseases. It is transmitted through blood and bodily fluids, and can be passed from mother to infant during pregnancy.

Amnesty International
Humanitarian organization established in the United Kingdom in 1961. It operates in over 150 countries and works to guarantee the civil rights and humane treatment of political prisoners around the world. It releases an annual report on the global human rights situation.

Artificial satellite
Vehicles created to be launched into orbit around the Earth or another planet. Satellites can be unmanned and remote-controlled from Earth, or fit for habitation and equipped with guidance systems on board. Depending on their use, satellites are categorized as telecommunication, meteorological, navigational, astronomic, scientific, military, or tele-survey satellites.

B

Biotechnologies
Genetic manipulation techniques using biological cells and their derivatives. They are applied in different sciences: microbiology, chemistry, biochemistry, genetics, and immunology. In agriculture and animal husbandry, they are the selection and cross-breeding techniques that improve or change vegetable and animal species to make them, for example, more resistant to disease, more profitable, or have higher protein content.

Birthrate
The number of births which occur in one year per every one thousand people. Also *birth index*.

Bit
Short for *Binary digit*, it is the minimum-sized unit of information, using only two numbers (0 and 1) to create all its codes. A group of eight bits forms a *Byte*. A *Megabyte* corresponds to 1,048,576 (2 to the power of 20) bytes. A *Gigabyte* corresponds to 1,024 (2 to the power of 10) Megabytes (or 2 to the power of 30 bytes). B*it/second* represents a channel's capacity, i.e. the quantity of information which can be transmitted through that channel in one second.

C

Capital flight
Export of capital in search of more profitable or safer investments in financial institutions or production activities in other countries. The flight of capital is illegal if there are bans (usually quantitative limits) on the export of financial resources.

Capitalism
Economic system characterized by the private or corporate ownership of property, production, and distribution resources. It relies on wage earners as workers, profit incentive, competition, and the free market.

Cartel
An alliance between companies belonging to the same production sector, who strive to achieve a monopoly of the market by limiting their mutual competition. Through cartels, companies manage to impose higher prices. One of the best-known cartels is the Organization of the Petroleum Exporting Countries (OPEC) which unites many oil producing countries.

Chip
A complex of electronic micro-circuits, used as a computer microprocessor, consisting of a small silicon plate

on which millions of transistors have been printed. Each transistor can carry out a vast number of logical operations per second. The chip production cost is small compared to their potential and their functions. Also *microchip* and *integrated circuit*.

Cold War

The global standoff which developed after World War II between the communist block and the Western democratic/capitalist world. The Cold War ended with the financial, military, and political demise of the Union of Soviet Socialist Republics (USSR) after a number of its republics, including Poland, Latvia, and Estonia, regained their independence. This communist country was formally dissolved on December 31, 1991.

Consumerism

The practice, which spread after the 1960s in most developed countries, of buying increasing amounts of nonessential and luxury goods. Fed by advertising and by goods that were manufactured to be replaced or consumed (rather than repaired or reused), this trend is so widespread that modern societies are called "consumer societies." It has been encouraged because of the theory that when people buy increasing amounts of goods, a country's economy grows and improves.

D

Data bank

A collection of information that is easily retrieved, updated, or modified. Data banks became an essential part of the computerized information revolution of the late 20th century. Data banks encompass all branches of knowledge, providing access to selected and organized groups of information which would otherwise be scattered, inconsistent, or inaccessible. Online banks all over the world can be accessed directly through Internet connections from a computer. Data banks can also be saved on optical discs (CD-ROM).

Debt service

The overall amount of capital repayments and interest on total debt paid by a debtor to a creditor, including payments between countries.

Demographic dynamics

Population variation due to the increase or drop in the number of people living in a given area, as well as to their emigration or immigration.

Demography

The science that studies the features of human populations using statistical methods.

Developing countries (DC)

A term created in the 1970s by international institutions to indicate countries whose economic structures were less developed than the richest countries. This replaced the word "underdeveloped," which could be interpreted as derogatory, and "Third World," which was no longer accurate.

E

Economic crisis

Disruption of balance between demand and supply of goods and services, causing a depression in the economic situation or in a specific sector or region.

Economy

All the monetary activities of a country and the amount of its yearly production. Economy also refers to the science which studies the rules of production, distribution and consumption of goods, and monetary flow within a specific economic system.

E-mail *(also email, electronic mail)*

The message sending and receiving system for individual users of a computer network. E-mail is an important step forward from paper mail, as it ensures extremely fast transmission worldwide, from any e-mail service to any other, and allows transmission of any multimedia document as an attachment.

Emigration

Permanent or temporary move of individuals or groups of people from one territory to another for business, political, personal, or religious reasons.

European Union (EU)

The inter-government organization first established in 1957 under the name of European Economic Community (EEC) by six Western European countries (Belgium, France, Germany, Italy, Luxembourg and the Netherlands), which was later joined by Denmark, Ireland, and the United Kingdom (1973), Greece (1981), Spain and Portugal (1986), and Austria, Finland, and Sweden (1995). On November 1,1993, the EEC became the European Union (EU), with the entry into force of the Maastricht Treaty, signed on the 7th of February 1992. Its objectives are: European citizenship, full economic and monetary union, and cooperation in foreign, judicial, security and police-related matters.

F

Food and Agriculture Organization of the United Nations (FAO)

The UN Food and Agriculture Organization was established in 1945 to increase food production, improve the distribution and trade of agricultural products, and increase the standards of living of rural people and the population in general. It is based in Rome, Italy.

Fax

A machine which can receive and send copies (facsimiles) of documents through telephone lines. A fax also refers to the paper document that results from such a transmission.

Fertility

The number of children a woman gives birth to during her fertile years (generally, between ages 15 and 49). This can be measured and averaged in a fertility rate or index for any given group of people.

Forced emigration

The movement of people who are forced to leave their country or community because of political, religious, or racial persecution, or because of wars or violence.

Foreign debt

The borrowing by all economic players of a country from other countries. It is difficult to determine, as today money circulates quite freely. Foreign debt, therefore, usually refers only to public foreign debt.

Functional illiteracy

The condition of those who, though able to read and write at a minimal level, cannot use these skills in modern society (for example, they cannot understand user instructions, complete bank transactions accurately, or read product labels with understanding).

G

Gender Development Index (GDI)

A list developed by the UN Development Program to record and compare gender equality results achieved in three criteria: life expectancy, education level, and decent standard of living.

Globalization

The world-wide spread of economic and financial processes, products, information, and culture. Fostered by increasingly fast and efficient media, such as Information Technology (IT) networks and satellite television, the globalization process is promoted by highly technologically and financially developed countries, which reap the greatest benefits. The term also refers to the inclusion of the entire world into a single integrated economic system dominated by multinational companies which operate on the world market with production units located in different countries.

Green revolution

The program promoted by the FAO in the 1970s to increase food production in underdeveloped countries. Based on the cultivation of high-yield dwarf species (mainly wheat and rice), it also entailed a greater use of chemical fertilizers.

Greenpeace International

The environmentalist association established in Canada in 1971 to coordinate world campaigns against nuclear power and for the safeguard of the environment and endangered species. Officially recognized by the United Nations, Greenpeace is based in Amsterdam, The Netherlands and has branch offices in 32 countries across all continents.

Gross Domestic Product (GDP)

The yearly ratio between the real economic growth of a country (regardless of the increase in prices) and the number of inhabitants. It is obtained by adding together the added value of the various economic sectors.

Gross National Product (GNP)

The GDP plus the remittances from citizens working abroad and the income of residents derived from investments abroad, after deduction of the remittances from foreign workers living in the country and the profit from foreign capital invested in the country. In small countries or countries whose economy is heavily dependant on foreign products, the difference between GDP and GNP can be considerable.

H

Humanitarian aid

Aid given by the international community (countries, organizations, associations) to the victims of natural disasters, armed conflicts, or serious political, economic, or social crises. Aid consists of goods and services (for instance, food, drugs, vaccines, water, clothes, shelter, psychological support, land mine removal, rehabilitation). Aid can also be preventive, as in the planting of trees against flooding. The objective of humanitarian aid is to prevent or relieve human suffering. Ideally, it is granted regardless of the victims' race, religion, gender, age, citizenship or political affiliation.

I

Illiteracy

The inability to read or write. The illiteracy rate is the percentage of people over the age of 15 who cannot read or write within the total population of a region.

International Monetary Fund (IMF)

An organization established in Washington, D.C. in 1945, to promote international cooperation in international monetary and currency stabilization, and to grant loans to the member countries experiencing a deficit in their balance of payments. The IMF plays a delicate and controversial role, especially in relation to the international debt of developing countries. The original 45 members have increased to today's 182.

Infant mortality

The number of children who die in their first year per every 1,000 live newborns in one year. Also *infant mortality rate or index*.

Inflation

General increase in prices resulting in a drop in a given currency's purchasing power.

Information Technology (IT)

The science involving all aspects related to the treatment of information through computers.
The term also indicates all technologies used for the processing, saving, use, and transfer of information used by a company, individuals, or a society.

International aid

Aid granted by industrialized countries or international organizations to underdeveloped countries in order to foster their development. It can consist of loans and donations, technical and scientific support, or international commercial benefits. Also *aid for development*.

International debt

The sum of public and private debt in developing countries, expressed in U.S. dollars or Swiss francs, Euros, or other currencies. Its value varies, depending on fluctuations in money exchange markets.

Internet

The system of interconnected computer networks using the TCP/IP (*Transmission Control Protocol/Internet Protocol*) transmission protocol. The Internet's rapid growth in the last decades of the 20th century created a new world-wide communication system, connecting millions of users from all countries. It has become universal thanks to its low costs, full anonymity, no clearly-defined ownership, and multiple uses, including private and public communication, information, business, trade, electronic mail, and data banks.

L

Labor productivity

The ratio between the value or quantity of the products manufactured and the value or quantity of the labor employed in production (number of employed and/or worked hours).

Labor supply

All individuals who are willing to work, or the number of hours that a country's population can offer.

Least Developed Countries (LDC)

That group of countries that the United Nations and the international community consider particularly weak in terms of economic and social development and having very low per capita incomes. Among these countries, the LIFDC (*Low Income Food Deficit Countries*) have populations which also suffer serious undernourishment. Also LIC (*Low Income Countries*)

Leptospirosis

An infectious disease which is widespread across the world. It is caused by the bacteria passed in urine from infected animals (mice, pigs) into water and mud, which then come into contact with the human body through the skin

Life expectancy

The average number of years that a person living in a given country may expect to live. It is an important indicator of the level of development and wealth of the population.

M

Mass media

All means (including newspapers, magazines, radio, television, movies, and posters) of disseminating messages and news to a very high number of receivers. Mass media have great importance in modern society, as they not only ensure a far-reaching spread of information, but can also be used to manipulate information for vested interests (by political parties, associations, commercial groups, and lobbies) or to promote behavioral and consumption models or gain consensus of public opinion.

Metropolis

A very large city, playing a leading role in the economic, political, administrative or cultural life of a country. The aggregation of several metropolitan districts forms a *megalopolis*.

Microsoft

U.S. IT company established in 1975 by Bill Gates and Paul Allen. It created the MS-DOS and Windows operating systems, whose success made it the world leader in the personal computer software sector.

Monopoly

A form of manufacturing or market where products are in the hands of one single company or where there is only one seller. The lack of competitors in a monopoly favors the monopolist, who fixes the price. This hurts consumers and potential competitors, so many countries apply antitrust laws and standards (*antitrust policies*) to limit monopolies.

Mortality rate
The number of deaths taking place over a certain time-span (usually one year) per every 1,000 people. Also *mortality index*.

Multinational company
A company carrying out its production and selling activities in various countries through branches or subsidiaries.

N

Natural growth
Population growth deriving simply from the difference between births and deaths.

Natural population change
The difference between the number of births and deaths occurring in one population in one year. It is positive if the number of births exceeds the number of deaths. It is negative in the opposite case.

Network
A connected group of private television stations, usually belonging to a single owner and broadcasting over the entire national territory. Also a series of computers interconnected in order to exchange data.

Non-governmental Organization (NGO)
All organizations of volunteers who work to provide aid or to raise public awareness and collect funds for aid.

Nutrition
All physiological processes through which living beings take food, transform it, and use it for their physical growth and as an energy source to carry out their activities.

O

Organization of the Petroleum Exporting Countries (OPEC)
This organization was established in Baghdad (Iraq) in 1960 to coordinate a common policy for oil production and trade. It includes Algeria, Saudi Arabia, the United Arab Emirates, Indonesia, Iran, Iraq, Kuwait, Libya, Nigeria, Qatar, and Venezuela.

P

Population aging
The increase in the percentage of elderly people (over 65 years) in the overall population of a region.

Population density
The ratio between the number of people living in a specific territory and the territory surface, expressed in people/sq mile (km).

Primary sector
That part of an economy which includes all economic activities based on the direct exploitation of living resources, such as agriculture, forestry, farming, hunting, and fishing.

Privatization
The process whereby the control and management of economic activities are transferred from the government to private companies.

Protectionism
An economic policy which, through customs duties and other measures, supports domestic companies by protecting them from competition from the imports of goods manufactured abroad.

Protein
An organic substance consisting of chains of interconnected amino acids. Proteins play a crucial role for the cell structures and functions in all living creatures and form the molecular entities through which genetic information is expressed. Also *protide*.

Public debt
The sum of the domestic and foreign money that the government and public institutions owe to others. It can be gross (the sum of all debts) or net (if credits are deducted).

Q

Quality of life
The concept that attempts to describe and measure the level of well being achieved in human activities.

R

Refugee
A person who leaves his/her country of origin in order to flee the risk of being persecuted because of his/her race, religion, nationality, specific social group, or political opinion.

Right of asylum
The right that a person in a dangerous situation in their own country has to apply for personal protection from the government of another country. Because of this right, after their situation has been examined, applicants acquire the status of refugees. During the time when the person is an "asylum applicant" the protection of the "*non refoulement*" (non-rejection) principle applies.

S

Self-sufficiency
The ability of a nation to produce enough to meet the basic needs of its population. Also the ability of a person to meet his or her own needs without external assistance.

Shanty town
A district on the outskirts of a large city, consisting of huts (shanties) where destitute people live. Shanty towns are called *bustees* in India, *favelas* in Brazil, *callampas* in Chile, *gourbevilles* in Tunisia, and *villas miserias* in Argentina.

Silicon Valley
A region south of San Francisco, California, where, starting in the 1930s, the first technopolis in the world developed. Silicon is the element used to build microprocessors. Today the Silicon Valley is home to the leading electronic companies in the world.

Software
All programs, instructions, and languages that, once entered, enable a computer to perform all its functions, as opposed to hardware, which refers to the material, electrical, and mechanical components making up the computer.

Sub-Saharan Africa
The whole region of the African continent south of the Sahara Desert.

T

Temporary work
A type of employment whereby companies are able to use the services of one or more workers recruited by an employment agency, on a day-to-day or weekly basis, without benefit of a long-term employment contract. It is very common in the United States, Great Britain, and France. Also *employee leasing*.

Tourism balance
The ratio between the income produced by foreign tourism in a given country and the money spent abroad by that country's citizens for tourism.

Trade balance

The relationship between all imports and exports of goods that a country has with foreign countries with which it has commercial relations. It is "even" when the total value of imported goods equals that of exported goods.

Transistor

A semi-conductor device fitted with three electrodes, whose electrical resistance can be varied within specific ranges. Conceived by J. Bardeen, W.H. Brattain, and W.B. Shockley in 1947, transistors have been widely applied as amplifiers, detectors, and switches, because they offer solidity, very limited encumbrance, no heating filament, and low energy consumption. They are the main components of all modern electronic appliances, both analogical (signal amplifiers) and digital (microprocessors, and logical circuits in general).

U

Underdeveloped area

An area that has chronically poor economic and social conditions.

Unemployment rate

The ratio between the number of unemployed and the overall work force in a country or territory.

Uneven exchange

This refers to a country's export of raw materials (with low-added value) and the import by the same country of finished products (with high-added value). This economic system is based on a single type of production aimed at exports, and makes the nation dependent on foreign countries to meet many of its population's needs for those things its country does not produce.

United Nations (U.N.)

The most important of all international organizations, established in 1945 to maintain peace and security in the world and promote economic, social, and cultural cooperation. It includes almost all nations.

United Nations Development Program (UNDP)

Based in New York City, this international organization, established in 1966, fosters economic progress in developing countries through projects and funds.

United Nations Educational Scientific and Cultural Organization (UNESCO)

The United Nations Educational Scientific and Cultural Organization was established in London (England) in 1945 to promote cooperation in all countries through education, science, and culture. It is based in Paris, France.

Universal Mobile Telecommunications System (UMTS)

The European standard for telecommunications, defined by the ITU (*International Telecommunications Union*), which applies to third-generation (3G) multimedial telephones. It uses a broadband mode which can manage high-speed data transmission (10,000 times faster than the second generation GSM system), thus enabling the transfer of moving images, Internet connections, and high-fidelity sounds.

United Nations High Commissioner for Refugees (UNHCR)

Established in 1951 and based in Geneva (Switzerland), this UN agency aims at guaranteeing legal protection and material aid for refugees (people fleeing their home country for political, racial or religious reasons) on strictly humanitarian grounds. It attempts to ensure that they can go back to their homeland (when possible) or takes care of their accommodation in the hosting country. It received the Nobel Peace Prize in 1981.

United Nations International Children's Emergency Fund (UNICEF)

This subsidiary body of the UN General Assembly,

was set up in 1946 in New York City. It cooperates with governments to develop projects for the world's children, raises funds required for such projects, maintains health care services, promotes health campaigns, takes action in emergency situations or in case of food shortages or educational deficiencies, allocates funds for needy children worldwide, and funds initiatives aimed at training qualified staff for child care. Today, UNICEF operates in 161 countries all over the world, particularly in developing countries. It was awarded the Nobel Peace Prize in 1965.

Urban studies
The techniques and scientific disciplines that study the changes that the creation of cities causes to human society, the surrounding region, and the environment.

Urbanization
The spreading of elements of the urban landscape to rural areas (residential buildings, industrial and commercial activities, etc.). The *urbanization rate* or *index* represents the percentage of city dwellers against the total population of a given region or country.

Urbanism
A phenomenon whereby cities attract people living in rural areas, who flow to the cities, causing a population increase. This phenomenon is caused by various reasons, mainly economic, sociological and psychological motives.

V

Vaccination
Administration of a substance (vaccine) to a person or animal, in order to cause active immunization against a specific disease. Since organisms can acquire complete and long-term immunity to a disease after contracting and overcoming its infection, a similar immunity can be artificially created by injecting the infectious agents or their products (vaccines). The most important vaccinations are those against smallpox, poliomyelitis, diphtheria, tetanus, hepatitis B, measles, parotitis, rubella, whooping cough, tuberculosis, yellow fever, and cholera.

W

World Wide Web (www)
The world-wide network of Internet servers that enables the interactive use of multimedia information in real time. It also refers to the complex of Internet users and resources using the HTML (*Hyper Text Markup Language*) protocol.

World Health Organization (WHO)
The UN specialized organization created in 1946 to ensure that all peoples, particularly those living in developing countries, can reach the highest possible public health level and hygiene standards. It also promotes international cooperation in medical research. Its main activities include campaigns to eliminate the most serious mass epidemics (malaria, marsh fever, smallpox, AIDS). It is based in Geneva (Switzerland).

World Bank
This intergovernmental organization, set up in 1945 and based in Washington, D.C., promotes bank lending to developing countries with its own funds and funds from the financial market. It includes the International Bank for Reconstruction and Development (IBRD) and its subsidiaries, the International Development Association (IDA), and the International Finance Corporation (IFC).

Index